James R. Parsons

Prussian Schools Through American Eyes

A report to the New York state Department of public instruction. Third

Edition

James R. Parsons

Prussian Schools Through American Eyes
A report to the New York state Department of public instruction. Third Edition

ISBN/EAN: 9783337213299

Printed in Europe, USA, Canada, Australia, Japan

Cover: Foto ©Paul-Georg Meister /pixelio.de

More available books at **www.hansebooks.com**

PRUSSIAN SCHOOLS

THROUGH AMERICAN EYES

A Report to the New York State Department
of Public Instruction

—BY—

JAMES RUSSELL PARSONS, JR.,

LATE U. S. CONSUL AT AIX-LA-CHAPELLE (AACHEN)

SYRACUSE, N. Y. :
C. W. BARDEEN, PUBLISHER
1891

Copyright, 1891, by C. W. BARDEEN

PREFACE

This brief account of the Prussian elementary school system was prepared at the request of the Honorable Andrew S. Draper, Superintendent of Public Instruction for the State of New York, and appears in his thirty-seventh annual report, transmitted to the Legislature January 6, 1891.

The following extract from Superintendent Draper's report explains itself:—

In 1867, Superintendent Victor M. Rice presented to the Legislature a special and elaborate report, attempting to set forth the educational conditions of all the enlightened nations of the world. The little volume was published by the State, but the edition was so limited that it is now almost unknown. It enabled the educators of the State to compare their own with other educational systems, and it was likewise prolific of suggestions. Its value, however, was impaired by reason of the fact that the information it contained was derived from the reports of foreign educational or other officers, or from encyclopædias. To make them of the greatest value to us, foreign school systems must be seen through American eyes, and must be described by an intelligent friend of our school system, who is so anxious for its improvement that he is willing to seize upon any thing which will improve it, no matter where he may find it, and who yet has the power of discriminating sufficiently to enable him to see not only what is good, but to determine what is practicable and advisable in this country.

I have been desirous of presenting to the educators of this State something of this character covering the educational work of the leading nations of Europe, and of presenting it in such form as to make it available to all officers and teachers in the State. When, therefore, Mr. James Russell Parsons, Jr., of Hoosick Falls, the accomplished school commissioner of the first commissioner district of Rensselaer county from 1885 to 1888, was made United States Consul at Aix-la-Chapelle, Germany, it occurred to me that the opportunity was offered for making an excellent beginning in this direction. The Prussian elementary school system is the oldest, and admitted to be, in many regards, the best in the world. The man who could investigate and describe it more completely than most men in our State was going there to live for a considerable time, and to live under circumstances which would give him special facilities and opportunities for information. He readily acquiesced in my desire that he should undertake the work, and has presented me with a more comprehensive and detailed description of the plan of organization and the operations of the Prussian school system, in more compact form than any other which is available to American readers. It is herewith transmitted to the Legislature, to the end that it may appear in the annual report and reach all interested in the educational progress of the State, and in the confident belief that it will enable us to see more clearly the strong points and discern the weak points of our own system. If this undertaking shall seem to be pleasing and helpful, I hope to follow it next year with similar descriptions covering the public educational systems of England and France.

I may add that it seems to me altogether the clearest statement that has ever appeared in English of just what the Prussian schools are doing.

SYRACUSE, *March 9, 1891.*   C. W. BARDEEN.

CONTENTS

	PAGES
Introduction	1

FIRST CHAPTER.

Scope of Report	1–2
Maintenance of Elementary Schools, the State's first duty	2
Inferiorities of the New York Elementary School System	2–3
Superiorities of the Prussian Elementary School System	3–5
Qualifications of School Commissioners (*Kreisschulinspektoren*)	5–6
Other Supervising Officers	6
Recommendation for New York	6–7
Compulsory Education Laws	7–8
State Supervision of Private Schools	8
Uniform Courses of Study	8–9
The best results often obtained in Ungraded Schools	9
Expedient adopted to prevent a too frequent change of teachers upon promotions in Graded Schools	9
Length of School Terms and Vacations	9–10
Recommendation for New York—The Township System	10
Prussian Elementary Schools are free	10–11
Teachers' Wages	11–12
Total Cost of Public Education in Prussia	12–13

SECOND CHAPTER.

The German Script	13–15
Orthography	15
Dialects	15
Language used in teaching. Number of Children of school age in whose families only some language other than German is spoken	15–16
Other Language Work	16–17
Arithmetic	17
Geography	17
History	17
Natural History	17
Music	17–18
Physical Training	18
Industrial Training for Girls	18
Drawing	18–19
Training of Children in the love of the Fatherland	19

(v)

	PAGES
Text-Books	19–20
Apparatus used in teaching	20
Teachers' Libraries	20
Interest of the General Public in School Work	20

THIRD CHAPTER.

Religious Instruction. Brief Summary of principal decrees relating thereto	21–22
Division of Children of School Age in the Public Elementary Schools, according to Religious Faith, upon May 20, 1886.	22

FOURTH CHAPTER.

School-houses and Sites	23–26
Observations	26–27

FIFTH CHAPTER.

Institutions for Children under School Age. *Krippen-Kinderbewahranstalten-Kleinkinderschulen-Kindergärten*	27–28
Institutions for Children of School Age and older. *Gymnasien, Mittelschulen*—Asyla for Orphans, the Blind, Deaf and Dumb, Insane—Reform Schools—Elementary Schools proper.	28–31

SIXTH CHAPTER.

The normal divisions of Prussian Elementary Schools	31–32
Course of Study and Time-tables for Ungraded Schools	32–37
The Half-day School (*Halbtagsschule*)	38
Course of Study for Schools with Two Departments	38–43
The School with Three Classes and Two Teachers	43–45
The School with Three Classes and Three Teachers	45
The School with Four Departments	45–46
The School with Five Departments	46
The School with Six Classes	47–48
Table showing the Relative Distribution of Prussian Elementary Public Schools in 1886	48–49

SEVENTH CHAPER.

Schools preparatory to the Normal, for Males (*Präparandenanstalten*)	49–50
Course of Study	50–52

EIGHTH CHAPTER.

Normal Schools for Male Teachers	52–57
Syllabus of Work	57–60

NINTH CHAPTER.

First Teachers' Examination for Temporary License	60–62
Second and final Teachers' Examination	62–63

TENTH CHAPTER.

Normal Schools for Females	63–64

vii

	Pages
ELEVENTH CHAPTER.	
Examination of Female Teachers....	.64–66
TWELFTH CHAPTER.	
Special Certificates.....................	.66–67
THIRTEENTH CHAPTER.	
School Commissioners (*Kreisschulinspektoren*).	.67–72
Supervision of Schools in January, 1889....	73–74
FOURTEENTH CHAPTER.	
Teachers' Conferences.............	..74–75
FIFTEENTH CHAPTER.	
School Discipline and Miscellaneous Regulations	.75–78
Observations.........	78
SIXTEENTH CHAPTER.	
Appointment of Teacher's-Vacancy occasioned by the death of Teacher.............	78
Vacancies arising from other Causes..	78–79
The filling of vacancies through duly authorized Teachers...	79–80
The filling of vacancies temporarily through Candidates......	80
Substitutes during vacations and leaves of absence....	80
SEVENTEENTH CHAPTER.	
Leaves of Absence of Teachers...........................	80–81
Conclusion....	...81–82

PRUSSIAN ELEMENTARY SCHOOLS.

„Alle Kinder, reiche und arme, vornehme und geringe, Knaben und Mädchen, müssen in Schulen unterrichtet, in allen Kindern muss Gottes Ebenbild wieder hergestellt. Jedes muss für seinen künftigen Beruf befähigt werden."

Drs. Schneider and Petersilie.

INTRODUCTION.

Since 1816, Prussian common schools have been the best in the world. Though much has been done to unify the systems in other parts of the Empire, nevertheless Prussian schools must not be confounded to-day with other German schools.

Prussia has no code of public instruction. This fact makes it rather difficult to secure reliable general information. The material for this report was gleaned from many sources. The principal references are to the editions (1882-1884-1887) of Giebe's "*Verordnungen betreffend das gesammte Volksschulwesen in Preussen*;" "*Preussische Statistik 101*," Berlin, 1889; the school laws of 1885, 1887, 1888 and 1889 and various Prussian school journals and official statistics.

Several German states have general school laws. For some years Prussia has been considering the advisability of a general school code. At present, with the exception of a few general laws, the schools are regulated by governmental decrees, many of which are purely local and apt to prove misleading to the foreigner.

I feel it my duty to express gratitude for kindnesses extended to me by Prussian government officials, school officers and teachers. I am indebted particularly to Kreisschulinspektor Dr. Keller and Oberlehrer Dr. Krick of Aix-la-Chapelle, also Seminarlehrer Franz Hinsen of Linnich.

Prussia is divided into fourteen provinces, viz.: East Prussia, West Prussia, Brandenburg, Pomerania, Posen, Silesia, Saxony, Schleswig-Holstein, Hanover, Westphalia, Hessen-Nassau, Rhine, Berlin, Hohenzollern.

Each province is subdivided into government departments (*Regierungs-Bezirke*), thirty-six in number for the whole kingdom.

The *Regierungs-Bezirke* are again divided into circles, called *Kreise*. Finally the *Kreise* are subdivided into districts.

Each *Regierungs-Bezirke* has a Regency (*Regierung*), presided over by the *Regierungs-Präsident*, and each province has its *Oberpräsident* (head-president).

All the gradations of public instruction are adapted to this scale of administrators.

FIRST CHAPTER.

I. SCOPE OF REPORT.

The aim of the following report is to give, in a condensed form, from the standpoint of a New Yorker, the organization, classification and work accomplished in Prussian elementary schools properly so called. Other schools in which elementary work is done, such as the middle schools (*Mittelschulen*), are not touched upon except generally and as it becomes necessary in stating the qualifications of teachers and school commissioners.

The reader follows the would-be elementary school teacher through the elementary school, the school preparatory to the normal, the normal school and the final examinations.

An attempt is made to state clearly and concisely the minimum of work required of each Prussian child * and the provisions by which the accomplishment of this work is secured.†

II. MAINTENANCE OF ELEMENTARY SCHOOLS THE STATE'S FIRST DUTY.

In Prussia the support of the elementary schools is considered the first and most important duty of the State. Even in time of war these schools must not be closed. The teachers who have passed the final examination and received definite appointments are sure of their pay, even though the schools to which they are appointed cease to exist. Teachers in elementary schools are on the same footing with clergymen as regards freedom from the payment of taxes; they have but six weeks' instead of three years' military service, and for this time their wages as teachers and those of their substitutes as well must be paid. They are also freed from the duty of quartering soldiers in time of war. Finally, at the close of their active service, they draw pensions from the government.

III. INFERIORITIES OF THE NEW YORK ELEMENTARY SCHOOL SYSTEM.

When Prussia was defeated by the armies of the great Napoleon, she turned her attention toward the perfection of her system of education. At the close of the Franco-Prussian war, France followed the same course, which resulted in the adoption of the essential features of the elementary school system of Prussia.

The New Yorker, anxious for a high degree of perfection in the elementary schools of his State, must be struck forcibly by the following merits of the Elementary School System of Prussia. Furthermore, if sufficiently interested to push his investigations farther, he can test in France, under a republican form of government, the operations of laws assuring similar advantages:

1. *Compulsory education laws, necessitating a full and regular attendance of the children of school age.*
2. *Official courses of study fixing the work to be accomplished in each of the different grades of schools. Uniformity is thus secured in the work done in all schools of the same class.*

---

* The only exceptions, excluding those unfit for any intellectual training, are children mentally, morally or physically incompetent. The education of these children is cared for in special schools for dullards, reform schools and institutions for the deaf, dumb and blind. The stupid are brought as far as possible in the elementary school course, generally in regular schools, sometimes in special schools for dullards.

† "The Prussian law, which fixes a *minimum* of instruction for the elementary schools, likewise fixes a *minimum* of instruction for the middle schools (*Mittelschulen*); and there are two kinds of examination, extremely distinct, for obtaining the brevet of primary teacher for these two gradations. *The elementary instruction must be uniform and invariable, for the primary schools represent the body of the nation, and are destined to nourish and to strengthen the national unity.* This is not the case with the burgher schools, for these are designed for a class among whom a great many shades and diversities exist—the middle class. In Prussia these middle schools have, accordingly, very different gradations from the *minimum* fixed by the law." (Cousin.)

3. Definite qualifications and experience in teaching for eligibility to the office of school commissioner.
4. Provisions elevating teaching to the dignity of a profession and making the tenure of office secure.
5. Trained teachers in rural as well as city districts and a school year of at least forty weeks.
6. General supervision of instruction for children of school age in private schools and families, including the qualifications of instructors.

New York elementary schools will never compare favorably with those of Prussia without similar provisions. Until these provisions are secured, advanced schools are of secondary importance. The first duty of the State is to provide suitably for a good elementary school education.

As stated by M. Victor Cousin in 1833, primary instruction is too far advanced in Prussia to render it necessary to make very frequent reports on the subject.

Cousin reviewed carefully the state of primary instruction in Prussia in the year 1831, under the firm conviction that the experience of Germany, and particularly of Prussia, ought not to be lost upon the French people.

"*National rivalries or antipathies,*" said he, "*would here be completely out of place. The true greatness of a people does not consist in borrowing nothing from others, but in borrowing from all whatever is good, and in perfecting whatever it appropriates. I am as great an enemy as any one to artificial imitations; but it is mere pusillanimity to reject a thing for no other reason than that it has been thought good by others. With the promptitude and justness of the French understanding, and the indestructible unity of our national character, we may assimilate all that is good in other countries without fear of ceasing to be ourselves. * * * There are branches of the public service which must be secured against all casualties by the State, and in the first rank of these is primary instruction.*"

The suggestions of M. Cousin were followed in the main, though, it must be granted, after a long delay. In New York, once convinced of the necessity of reforms, we move with incredible celerity. It is interesting to note that the report of Cousin, published in 1833, emphasizes what are to-day the main defects of our system of primary instruction.

IV. SUPERIORITIES OF THE PRUSSIAN ELEMENTARY SCHOOL SYSTEM.

A careful observer of the work done in Prussian elementary schools will detect, naturally enough, many imperfections, and yet he will return to this country with the feeling that Prussia is far in the lead of us. Take as an example a wealthy school district in New York State where parents are alive to the advantages of a good education. Suppose, as is often the case with us, that teachers and supervising officers are thoroughly competent, that the length of the school year approximates that of the Prussian school year, and that the attendance of the children is regular. The work done in these schools is fully equal to that done in the best Prussian elementary schools. Unfortunately, however, up to the present time, such schools have been exceptions here and not the rule as in Prussia.

Our children learn as easily as the Prussian children, but under existing laws the pupils of the average New York school district, between the ages of 6 and 14, can not compete with the children of the average school district in Prussia. It is in vain that New York State goes on spending more and more each year for educational purposes. Without legislation insuring a full and regular attendance of the children of school age; without definite uniform qualifications for supervising officers as well as teachers; without an approximate equalization of local taxation for school purposes; without State supervision of instruction given in private schools and families, we shall never attain anything approaching uniformity in the work done in our elementary schools.

It is very unjust to make the sweeping assertion that no good elementary school work is done in New York State. I have visited many schools in countries of the old world as well as in New York, and have never seen better elementary schools anywhere in the world than the best schools here at home. Every Prussian child between the ages of 6 and 14* must, except in cases of severe illness or other extraordinary cause, be present at every session of the school he attends. The lists of the children of school age, in charge of the local police (in rural districts the Burgermeister), are kept so carefully that it is impossible to escape the provisions of the compulsory education laws, as much so as it is to evade the military service. Dispensations amounting to more than four weeks in the school year are never given to children under 12 years of age, and to them only when sickness in the family or other unusual cause make it advisable.† Even then such children must prove the attainment of a sufficient degree of proficiency in the work laid down by law for elementary schools. Examinations are held regularly to determine the pupils' ripeness in such work, and they may be forced to attend school beyond the close of the fourteenth year of age, when, through previous irregular attendance or lack of diligence, the results of the examination are not satisfactory. Pupils leaving elementary schools, before the close of the fourteenth year of age, to attend a higher school, must submit to the school commissioner a certificate from the director of such higher school. Again, should the pupil leave such higher school before having attained the age of 14, the director must notify the school commissioner a second time. In every province there are houses of correction for children of school age who can not be otherwise controlled. The school commissioner and *Landrath* decide as to the sending of children to these institutions. Unless the parents are very poor, they are forced to pay the costs. In 1885 there were 180 of these houses of correction (*Rettungshäuser*) in Prussia, 141 of which were established since 1848.‡

---

*Although the school age in some parts of the kingdom legally begins when children have attained the age of 5, yet, as a matter of fact, compulsory education laws are everywhere first enforced at the end of the sixth year of age and, except in certain districts, continue in force eight years.

"Thatsächlich wird überall das vollendete 6. Lebensjahr als Beginn der Schulpflicht behandelt, mit der Massgabe, dass in einigen Regierungsbezirken zu Ostern jeden Jahres auch solche Kinder aufgenommen werden, welche das 6 Lebensjahr erst bis zum 1. Juli, bez. 1. Oktober desselben Jahres vollenden. . . . . Die Schulpflichtigkeit besteht im Grossen und Ganzen für jedes vollsinnige Kind in Preussen thatsächlich rund acht Jahre." (Drs. Schneider and Petersilie.)

†Children under 12 years of age are forbidden to work in factories or mines. Those between 12 and 14 are restricted by law to six hours a day.

‡Between October 1, 1878 and March 31, 1886, 11,101 children were sent to these houses of correction ("*Statistisches Handbuch für den Preussischen Staat*," Berlin, 1888).

Would it not be very difficult to find many children of New York State who, between the ages of 6 and 14, had not absented themselves for long periods from school? With us most trivial excuses are accepted, and the time lost in these eight years is considerable. It is no wonder, then, that the Prussian children of 13 and 14 are, in general, far in advance of our children of the same age. In our cities and villages, however, where the school year approximates in length that which the Prussian decrees fix definitely for their elementary schools, I contend that the children are not as far behind as we should expect them to be, when we consider their irregularity in attendance.

V. QUALIFICATIONS OF SCHOOL COMMISSIONERS.

Within the past few years, much has been done to call the attention of the people to the essential defects in our school system. There has been a great improvement all along the line, and yet, with one exception, that of uniform qualifications and examinations for teachers' certificates, the most important defects are still to be remedied.

The teachers in our public schools must now attain a certain standard, and yet, contrary to the precedents established by other countries and contrary to reason, the officers who supervise the work of these teachers, the school commissioners, have but one qualification, as the *sine qua non*, that is, ability to secure a plurality of the votes cast at a popular election. There are many thoroughly efficient school commissioners in the State. Under existing laws, however, these cases may be considered as accidents. The inefficient officers worry the teachers whose educational qualifications are far superior to their own; add an immense amount of unnecessary work to the Department of Public Instruction; and make our school system a laughing-stock to other countries where such inconsistencies are unknown.

In order to understand the qualifications required of school commissioners (*Kreisschulinspektoren*) in Prussia, let us review briefly the requirements of male teachers. 1. *Elementary schools.* It may be stated at the outset that almost all the male elementary school teachers are normal school graduates. To insure similarity in training and a thorough knowledge of character, few foreigners and few beside normal school (*Schullehrer-Seminar*) graduates are admitted to the male teaching force. From 6 to 14 the would-be teacher has attended, let us suppose, an elementary school. He must then absolve the three years' course laid down for the preparatory schools (*Präparanden-Anstalten*). These preparatory schools (*Präparanden-Anstalten*) are special institutions which fit for the normal (*Schullehrer-Seminar*). He is now ready for the normal school. At the close of a three years' course at the normal school he is admitted to the first teachers' examination. If successful, he must next practice as candidate or assistant teacher not less than two years and not more than five years before his admission to the final test (*Zweite Prüfung*). It is a most excellent idea to defer this final test until the applicant has been tried in the school-room. In this way only can decision be reached as to teaching capacity, discipline, etc. If teacher fails to pass the examination within five years, he is dropped. 2. *Middle schools.* For teachers of lower classes the same requirements with the addition of ability to teach a foreign tongue, or natural history in its broadest sense, and the attainment of the mark "good" in all subjects at the final examination (*Zweite Prüfung*). For higher classes, a special examination provided for middle school teachers (*Prüfung der Lehrer an Mittelschulen*). There is really no gradation between elementary and middle schools. The latter merely go on somewhat further with elementary school work, introducing French, Latin and English. 3. *High schools* (*Realschulen, Realgymnasien, Progymnasien and Gymnasien*). All high school teachers, except those engaged in technical departments, must first absolve the nine years' gymnasial course, which commences at the close of the third school year. Next comes the university course of three or four years. The candidate is now ready for the State examination. The subjects for this State examination (*Staatsprüfung*) are divided into four classes: 1. The ancient languages and German; 2. Mathematics and natural sciences; 3. History and geography; 4. Religion and Hebrew. At the close of one years' practice to test teaching capacity, he receives a second certificate and is thereupon engaged provisionally. On account of strength of competition he is often forced to wait as many as six years before receiving a permanent position. The advancement to the position of head master (*Oberlehrer*) follows generally in Prussia, after the twelfth year of service, always providing that the teacher has done well in the State examination and has also been successful in teaching. 4. *Normal school teachers and directors;* directors of schools preparatory for the normal; directors of middle schools and higher schools for girls (*Töchterschulen*) must pass a special examination provided for those who are to hold such positions (*Prüfung der Rectoren*).

The school commissioners (*Kreisschulinspektoren*) are either former regular high school teachers, generally doctors of philosophy, or more rarely theologians, or former normal school teachers. All must have had practical experience in teaching. It is not regulated by law how long they must have taught, but to insure efficiency, before permanent appointment as school commissioner, they are engaged provisionally for six months or longer. As with us, school commissioner districts vary greatly in size and in number of schools.

VI. OTHER SUPERVISING OFFICERS.

In addition to the school commissioners (*Kreisschulinspektoren*), there are (2) local school inspectors, generally the clergyman or mayor; (3) boards of education, consisting of the local school inspector, local officials and from two to four citizens; there is no salary attached to these offices; and (4) the government school councilors (*Regierungsräthe und Schulräthe*); and (5) *Landräthe*. The *Kreisschulinspektor* corresponds to our school commissioner. The other officers may be compared with our (2) and (3) school trustees and boards of education, (4) State department members (5) supervisors.*

VII. RECOMMENDATION FOR NEW YORK.

The uniform examinations for teachers' certificates are now definitely established in New York. No person should be eligible to the office of school commissioner who does not hold a teacher's license

---

* Prussian schools excepting *Fortbildungsschulen* (for young workmen and apprentices), which are under the jurisdiction of the minister of commerce, are controlled by the minister of education at Berlin through the provincial school consistories (*Provinzialschulcollegien*), provincial and district governments.

of the first grade or its equivalent, and who has not, in addition, practical experience as a teacher. In this way, we should establish at least a *minimum* of qualifications for this important office.

VIII. COMPULSORY EDUCATION LAWS.

The necessity for effective compulsory education laws has been thoroughly canvassed in this State. We understand fully the legal provisions made by other countries in this respect. New York is most generous towards her public schools. Every year the expenses of these schools are increasing. From $5,735,460.24 in 1865, the grand total for 1889 was $16,691,178.24, a sum nearly equal to one-sixth the total annual cost of the maintenance of the immense standing army of the German Empire or to one-third the annual cost of public education in Prussia. We are, as a people, most generous, and yet we are always anxious to get the worth of our money. Our public schools are for the people. Here, if anywhere, under a government by the people and for the people, an elementary school education is a matter of necessity. All the children between fixed ages should be forced to improve the educational advantages the state offers. In this way only can we make good and intelligent citizens of the rising generation.

Compulsory education laws are most effective in Prussia, as will be seen from the fact that for some years, the average number of recruits to the army, without elementary school training, has not exceeded two per cent, and in many parts of the kingdom has been less than two-tenths of one per cent. The most favorable statistics come from Hohenzollern, Schleswig-Holstein, Hanover, Berlin, Westphalia and Saxony; the most unfavorable from the eastern borders.

The following published by the Prussian bureau of statistics in 1889, are the latest available figures based upon the census of 1885 (Dec. 1).*

(1) Number of children between 5 and 6 years of age.... 679,267
(2) Number of children between 6 and 14 years of age.. 5,225,891

5,905,158

All those under (2) and a portion of those under (1) were subject to the compulsory education laws.

The number attending public elementary schools.	4,838,247
The number attending public middle schools, private schools, etc....	299,280
The number excused from attendance under legal provisions.	170,439
The number excused by reason of mental and physical infirmities	13,519
The number excused through lack of school accommodations	8,826
The number of cases of truancy reported	3,145

5,333,456

* The official statistics contained in "*Preussische Statistik 101*," Berlin, 1889, follow those published in 1878 and 1882. They give a complete picture of the elementary schools upon May 20, 1886. More than two years were expended in the compilation and tabulation of these statistics. Complete statistics of 1890 will not be published in all probability before 1892.

Including the 679,267 between 5 and 6 there remain 571,702 to be accounted for. But only a small proportion of these children were subject to the compulsory education laws, and furthermore, many between 12 and 14 were freed from the operation of these laws. It is clear that only a very small and inconsiderable fraction escape. Only 3,145 cases of evasion were reported and 8,826 where pupils were unable to gain admission directly through lack of school accommodations, a number less than in the city of New York alone.

IX. STATE SUPERVISION OF PRIVATE SCHOOLS.

As regards State supervision of private schools in the matter of qualifications of teachers and courses of study in the common school branches for pupils of school age, comparatively little has been said or written in this State. This discussion, however, will surely follow the enforcement of compulsory education laws. Before going abroad, I had often thought of this question in reflecting upon some of our inefficient private schools. High tuition bills are far from indicating a high grade of instruction. Fortunately, most of our private schools are very good. The patrons of all these schools and all interested therein should be willing to advocate that the teachers in private schools throughout the State possess at least the qualifications of teachers in public schools. This is the provision made abroad, and I have learned to appreciate its value.

Under compulsory education laws, the State fixes a *minimum* of work to be accomplished and a given time in which it is to be done. It then becomes the duty of the State to overlook all institutions where this elementary instruction is imparted. Private schools should be tested by the State to see if this *minimum* be attained. In all matters of opinion or in all work which is not laid down by the State, these schools should enjoy perfect freedom. If, however, New York is opposed to State supervision of private schools, uniformity in elementary school work may be secured by fixing the qualifications of private school teachers and compelling pupils to pass annual examinations in the work laid down by the State. Instruction given in families could be regulated in the same way. Compulsory education, to be efficient, necessitates a high degree of carefulness. There should be no loop-holes and nothing should be left to chance, if we desire uniformity in our elementary school work.*

X. UNIFORM COURSES OF STUDY.

The work to be accomplished in each Prussian elementary school is definitely laid down by law. Each school is not a law unto itself as to what shall be done and when and how this is to be done. I have

---

* "Whoever wishes to set up a private school must be subject to only two conditions, from which no school, public or private, can on any pretext be exempt — the brevet of capacity, given by the commission of examination, and the supervision of the committee of the *commune* and of the inspector of the department." (Cousin.)

Private elementary schools in Prussia are decreasing in number as the following table shows:

	City schools.		Rural schools.	
	1871.	1886.	1871.	1886.
Number of schools	1,382	894	486	315
Number of classes	3,744	3,266	737	517
Number of pupils	93,720	68,698	13,401	8,438

In 1886, there were also 961 private middle schools with 68,373 pupils.

learned by practical experience that the work in ungraded schools compares most favorably with that of graded schools. The courses of study vary little except as regards division of time and classes. The reader will note this by a comparison of the courses of study for ungraded schools and schools with two departments. Indeed, inasmuch as the courses of study of schools with more classes would have involved a repetition of the same work, I have given only the division of time and general regulations for these schools.

XI. THE BEST RESULTS OFTEN OBTAINED IN UNGRADED SCHOOLS.

Upon first visiting Prussian elementary schools, I heard the statement from school commissioners that the most thorough and systematic work is often done in ungraded schools. Whatever the standard of literary qualifications may be, some teachers will lack teaching capacity, and though Prussia is very careful in practical tests of teaching capacity, nevertheless even there some incompetency will creep in. A good teacher in an ungraded school, after having had the same children eight years, will often do better work than that done in graded schools where children change teachers upon promotion to another department. In this State, however, it would be very difficult to find many ungraded schools taught by the same teacher for the period of eight years.

XII. EXPEDIENT ADOPTED TO PREVENT A TOO FREQUENT CHANGE OF TEACHERS UPON PROMOTIONS IN GRADED SCHOOLS.

Teachers are often promoted with their classes, so that they instruct the same class three or four years. In exceptional cases, where teachers are incompetent, this plan works great injustice. Generally speaking, it is advantageous both for pupils and teachers.

XIII. LENGTH OF SCHOOL TERMS AND VACATIONS.

An examination of the decrees regulating the length of vacations in different government districts shows a difference of from one to three weeks in the time elementary schools remain in session annually. Forty-two weeks is the *minimum*, forty-five weeks the *maximum*. The hours of instruction per week vary in primary and advanced divisions from twenty to thirty-two, as will be seen by reference to courses of study.* In the government districts of Magdeburg and Hanover, the elementary schools are open at least forty-three weeks annually. Patriotic festivals, viz., the Emperor's birthday and the anniversary of Sedan, and general religious festivals not occurring in regular vacations are included. Patriotic festivals are celebrated by appropriate exercises in the schools. In Jewish schools, the vacations are arranged to include the Jewish festivals.† The length of the school year for Romanists, Protestants and Jews is substantially the same. Instead of taking Saturday, as with us, Prussian elementary schools are closed Wednesday and Saturday afternoons. Upon these half-days there is no instruction except as it may be necessary to fill out the time required for gymnastics and manual training.

---

*Half-day schools and schools with three classes and two teachers give only twelve hours instruction weekly in the lowest division.
†In Düsseldorf, sixteen holidays are allowed for the Jewish festivals. Those not falling in regular vacations must be made up, when exceeding the number of holidays in other schools.

The rural elementary schools in the government district of Potsdam are in session forty-two and fifty-seven hundredths weeks annually, the city and suburban schools forty-two and twenty-nine hundredths. The following serves to show when the vacations occur:

City and suburban schools.

	Days.
1. Easter	14
2. Whitsuntide	4
3. Summer vacation	28
4. Michaelmas	8
5. Christmas and New Year	14
	68

Rural schools.

1. Easter	10
2. Whitsuntide	4
3. Summer vacation	42
4. Christmas and New Year	10
	66

In addition to the religious holidays under 1, 2 and 5, and 1, 2 and 4, the government recognizes two common to Romanists and Protestants and seven peculiar to the Romanists.

Private schools must follow the rules of public schools for the districts to which they belong.

XIV. RECOMMENDATION FOR NEW YORK.

In 1889, the average length of time the schools of New York were in session was thirty-five and five-tenths weeks. The Prussian children gain from six to ten weeks a year. The township system, by equalizing local taxation, would enable us to increase the legal school year to at least forty weeks.

XV. PRUSSIAN ELEMENTARY SCHOOLS ARE FREE.

In this respect Prussia has passed through three stages. Under the first elementary schools were entirely self-supporting; under the second they received State aid, but were still largely self-supporting; under the third, Laws of 1888 and 1889, elementary schools were made free and the State pays a larger proportion of the cost of maintenance. Districts must pay for repairs, new buildings and cost of heating. If unwilling to provide proper school accommodations for the children of school age, they can be forced by the government to do so. Poor districts may receive special government aid to meet such expenses.*

In France the elementary schools are not only gratuitous, but books, paper, ink and school supplies generally are provided free of charge. More than this, the children of indigent parents are furnished with warm food in winter, with shoes and with clothing. In Prussia books

---
* In some districts the State pays the entire cost of maintaining the elementary schools. In other districts, excepting a small portion of teachers' salaries, the State pays nothing.

and school supplies are free only for the poor, who are also provided with food and clothing, that they may be enabled to attend school. Each district has its *caisse*, the revenues of which depend upon government and district grants or assessments made upon large landholders.

XVI. TEACHERS' WAGES.

The direct aim of the laws of June 14, 1888, and March 31, 1889, was to lighten the burden of local taxation for schools for children of school age. These laws have had a beneficial effect in increasing slightly the wages of teachers.

Teachers' salaries are still quite small in Prussia, particularly in the case of females. Allowances are generally made for house-rent and fuel. Teachers in rural districts are provided with a house and garden. Their salaries are often not much more than half those paid city teachers of the same grade, and yet, as regards professional training and character of work, they are fully equal to city teachers. It must be borne in mind, however, that city life is, as a rule, far more expensive than country life.

In comparing with salaries paid in New York, several things are to be considered.
1. The great difference in the purchasing power of money.
2. The absolute security of the teacher in his position.
3. The fact that he draws a pension of from one-fourth to three-fourths of his salary upon his retirement, the amount depending upon the number of years of official service.*

As the following table shows the average annual salary received by teachers in Prussia in 1886 was $267.50. The average for the same year in New York was $409.27. The Prussian teacher, however, received fuel and dwelling free, in addition to his regular salary.

Table A, taken from "*Preussische Statistik 101*," published at Berlin in 1889, shows the increase in teachers' wages in elementary schools from 1820 to 1886. Hohenzollern and the new provinces are not included.

Table A.

	City schools.	Country schools.	Together.
Number of teachers, 1820.	3,745	18,140	21,885
Number of teachers, 1878.	15,444	29,912	45,386
Number of teachers, 1886.	18,937	33,106	52,043
Average salaries, 1820†...	$159 50	$64 50	$80 75
Average salaries, 1878.....	354 25	238 25	276 75
Average salaries, 1886.....	319 25	237 75	267 50

Small as these averages are for 1886, nevertheless they are about three and one-half times greater than in 1820. They are to be increased by the allowance made for fuel and rent.

---

* In 1886, there were 4,211 pensioned elementary teachers in Prussia. The average pension was $170.25 (681 marks); 49.89 per cent of all pensions was paid by the State.
† Reckoned at four marks to the dollar.

Table B, from the same source, shows the scale of salaries for 1886, excluding special teachers such as those of industrial training for girls, referred to under special teachers.*

Table B.	Per cent of teachers.
Salaries from $37.50 to $75.00†............................	00.02
Salaries from 75.00 to 112.50...........................	00.33
Salaries from 112.50 to 150.00...........................	05.08
Salaries from 150.00 to 187.50...........................	14.04
Salaries from 187.50 to 225.00...........................	21.74
Salaries from 225.00 to 262.50...........................	20.41
Salaries from 262.50 to 300.00...........................	12.85
Salaries from 300.00 to 337.50...........................	07.96
Salaries from 337.50 to 375.00...........................	05.84
Salaries from 375.00 to 412.50...........................	03.41
Salaries from 412.50 to 450.00...........................	02.86
Salaries from 450.00 to 487.50...........................	01.76
Salaries from 487.50 to 525.00...........................	01.35
Salaries from 525.00 to 562.50...........................	00.60
Salaries from 562.50 to 600.00...........................	00.64
Salaries from 600.00 to 637.50...........................	00.25
Salaries from 637.50 to 675.00...........................	00.39
Salaries from 675.00 to 712.50...........................	00.08
Salaries from 712.50 to 750.00...........................	00.04
Salaries above $750.00..................................	00.32

XVII. TOTAL COST OF PUBLIC EDUCATION IN PRUSSIA.

In 1885, the population of Prussia was 28,318,470, and the total cost of public education *per caput* was $1.7717. Drs. Schneider and Petersilie of Berlin, in "*Preussische Statistik 101*," published in 1889, reckon the total cost for 1888, excluding army and navy schools, at $50,192,857. This amount is divided as follows:

		Per caput.
Universities........................	$3,769,405 00	$0.1322
High schools and seminaries...........	6,940,119 00	0.2459
Elementary instruction...............	37,357,857 00	1.3187
Trade schools......................	2,125,476 00	0.0749
	$50,192,857 00	$1.7717

As will be seen, about three-quarters of the total outlay is for elementary instruction.

The sources from which these funds come are:

	Per cent.
(1) From the State..	31.05
(2) From districts (*Kommunalverbände*)....................	46.19
(3) From revenues, funds, etc.............................	22.76

---

* Salaries advance with years of service. Male teachers with an experience of from ten to thirty years are allowed $125, female teachers, $87.50. This allowance is called *Alterszulage*. In schools with two or more teachers, the scale of salaries advances by $37.50, the amount received depending upon experience in teaching.
† Reckoned at four marks to the dollar.

Of the total of $37,357,857 for elementary instruction, the State pays 25.11 per cent. This will be raised from one-fourth to one-third by the law of 1889.

With the excessive local burdens of the past, it is a significant fact that Prussia has nevertheless maintained a very high standard in all grades of schools. In New York, we can hope to accomplish this only through an approximate equalization of local taxation for school purposes.

In Prussia, elementary instruction is the first consideration. The resolution adopted by the national assembly (*Landtag*) December 22, 1870, is a good illustration of this. It was at the very crisis of the Franco-German war, yet the *Landtag* called on the government to increase the number of normal schools and the capacity of those already existing, and "thus to put an end to the practice of filling up teachers' vacancies by appointing unqualified individuals" (*Centralblatt für die gesammte Unterrichts-Verwaltung, Berlin, October, 1877*). The result of this call is seen by the fact that twenty-four new normal schools were founded between 1870 and 1876.

The following table shows that, as in New York, the total cost of elementary instruction in Prussia has increased very rapidly within the past twenty years:

1871	$13,487,713 81
1878	24,051,576 90
1886	30,338,779 76

It is interesting to note the sources from which these funds came:

	1871.	1878.	1886.
Tuition bills	$2,199,712 86	$3,083,411 20	$3,775,121 43
Local taxes and funds	10,298,670 95	18,007,078 80	23,159,266 43
From the State	689,330 00	2,955,086 90	3,404,391 90
	$13,487,713 81	$21,051,576 90	$30,338,779 76

Tuition bills are now done away with except in the case of nonresident pupils. The change thus brought about increased the amount given by the State to 25.11 per cent in 1888. As above stated, the law of 1889 will raise the percentage of State aid from one-quarter to one-third the total cost of elementary instruction.

SECOND CHAPTER.

I. THE GERMAN SCRIPT.

Upon first entering a Prussian elementary school, an American is struck forcibly with the amount of time wasted in learning the German written and printed characters. Mediaeval German schools were fortunate at least in not having this disadvantage to contend with.

The German script is a corruption of the Roman. Up to the twelfth century the Roman was in use by all Latin and German people. This was gradually corrupted by the monks, and the so-called German script is the result. Upon the invention of printing, this script was modified still further, giving birth to the German printed characters.

The children in the Prussian elementary schools are now forced to learn eight alphabets, while, in most all other civilized lands, it is found difficult enough to teach four. First come the German written capital letters, then the corresponding small letters. The pupils are next worried with the German printed alphabets, large and small characters. They have now learned four alphabets, the number taught in our elementary schools; but they have not yet finished their *Fibel*, the book corresponding to our Primer and First Reader, completed at the close of the second year of instruction. This *Fibel* contains two more alphabets, the Roman printed characters, large and small. The seventh and eighth alphabets, namely, the Roman written large and small letters, are taught sometimes in the third school year, but generally later. This depends largely upon the opinions of teachers and supervising officers touching the German and Latin script.

Many famous Germans, such as Jak. Grimm, Leibuitz, Wieland, Ew. v. Kleist, Bodmer, Ramler, Hoelty, Richard Wagner, have declared against the German script and printed characters. More than 100 university professors and 6,000 teachers have followed their example. Thousands of books, and scientific works very generally, are printed every year in Roman characters. Nevertheless, force of habit and a false feeling of patriotism have thus far enabled the so-called German alphabets to retain their position in the schools.

More than 250,000,000 of people use exclusively the Roman characters. They are understood throughout the civilized world. England, America, Italy, Spain and France dictate in these characters to all who would have business or other relations with them. Holland, Sweden, Denmark and Bohemia realize this fact, and are now returning to the purer forms, which were in use up to the twelfth century. In spite of the ardent defenders of this same movement, Germany hesitates, and thus preserves a very formidable barrier between herself and other civilized nations.

Every practical educator will see at once the importance of this question. Much time is wasted in learning 100 superfluous letters. These letters are studied before the pupil's handwriting is formed, and, between the German and the Roman script, it is difficult for him to write consistently.

In justice to the teaching of penmanship in Prussian elementary schools, one must admit that, in view of this great disadvantage, the results obtained are surprisingly good. The pupils write fully as well as our own. Later in life, however, when they have used both alphabets to a greater extent, confusion of the two is apt to follow. It is very easy for us to decipher the German script when written as it should be, but we must work very hard to read readily ordinary business or social correspondence. The teacher whose written work in the school-room has struck you most favorably will often write a letter, which, when cold, he himself would have difficulty in deciphering. As with us, the pupils imitate the careful written work of the teacher in the school-room, and, up to a certain age, there is little variety. When, however, the handwriting is fully formed, that individuality comes out which gives it a distinctive character. With this individuality the German associates a greater degree of illegibility than the American.

II. ORTHOGRAPHY.

The attention of the American turns naturally from penmanship to orthography. He notes that German words are not spelled as in his school days. Accustomed to uniformity in this respect, the question interests him at once.

The orthography or *Rechtschreibung*, as the Germans call it, now taught in the Prussian schools, dates from the beginning of the school year 1880-81. It differs enough from the orthography taught prior to this date to make it rather unsafe for a father to attempt to correct the work of his children. Some of my readers have sons who have told them they knew nothing about Latin because they did not understand a quotation with the Roman or Continental pronunciation. German parents run the risk of being told by their children that they can not spell, when they write, as they often do, contrary to the new system of orthography.

The movement toward reform in English orthography has stronger advocates than is generally supposed, both in America and England. In Germany, however, the movement in a corresponding direction is much more widely felt. Far from satisfied with the system now in use, the Germans seem to be drifting toward phonetic spelling. One of the greatest safeguards with them, as with us, comes from the lack of uniformity in the systems proposed.

III. DIALECTS.

Another disadvantage under which Prussian elementary schools labor arises from the prevalence of various dialects. The children of the common people, upon first entering school, often speak and understand only the dialect of their parents. This is especially true in manufacturing districts. Many teachers gave me graphic descriptions of the difficulties encountered in endeavoring to teach High German. So great are these dialectic differences, that it often seems at first like teaching a foreign tongue.

IV. LANGUAGE USED IN TEACHING.

Since 1889, except in the case of religious instruction in districts with a large foreign population, the German language has been used universally in teaching all subjects in Prussian elementary schools. Up to 1887, the Polish language was in use in schools made up of Poles, and up to April 1, 1889, pupils in North Schleswig were taught in the Danish language.

Statistics of 1886 show that ten and thirty-five-one-hundredths per cent of the total number of children in attendance upon public elementary schools spoke only the Polish language at home. The percentage of children in whose families German was the only language spoken, was eighty-six and fifty-eight-one-hundredths. In the families of the other thirteen and forty-two-one-hundredths per cent, either another language was spoken in addition to German, or only a foreign tongue.

Number of children in whose families only Polish was spoken.	500,315
Number of children in whose families only Sclavonic dialects were spoken.	31,473
Number of children in whose families only Danish was spoken.	24,088
Number of children in whose families only some language other than German was spoken.	4,049
Total	559,925
Number of children in whose families only German was spoken.	4,188,857
Number of children in whose families German and another language were spoken.	89,465
Total	4,838,247

From this we see that the difficulty of teaching more or less in a foreign tongue existed in 1886 in the case of quite a considerable percentage of the school children.

With children entirely ignorant of German, the difficulty will not be overcome before the third or fourth school year.

Special text and reference-books have been issued for schools with a large foreign population. Courses of study are modified to meet the needs of such schools, and teachers receive special training therefor.

The Prussian government moved very carefully in this matter. Experiments seemed to prove the advisability of adopting the German language generally, and reports show that the results are very satisfactory.

The experiments made before adopting exclusively the German language in schools made up of foreigners were most interesting. The Minister of Public Instruction conducted these experiments in person. It was everywhere found that children who had not spoken a single German word before entering school, not only made great progress in the elementary school *curriculum* when the instruction was given in German, but also expressed themselves best in their native tongue. The ministry was at last satisfied that it was advisable to adopt the German language exclusive of all others.

V. OTHER LANGUAGE WORK.

Other language work in Prussian elementary schools differs very little from that in New York, as will be seen by reference to the courses of study. In teaching reading, the use of the alphabet method is positively forbidden in all schools. More attention is paid, later in the course, to ordinary business forms than is the case generally with us. For example, the government has supplied each school with specimens of mail matter, such as envelopes, money-orders, parcel-express blanks, etc., and pupils are instructed carefully as to their uses. The same care is shown in drawing notes, bills, receipts, etc.

Another point worthy of mention is the instruction given in memorizing proverbs, aphorisms and selections in poetry and prose. This is pushed much further than with us.

Prussia sets us a good example in her elementary schools as regards the attention paid to German literature. In our elementary schools we do not succeed as well as the Prussians in cultivating a taste for good reading.

VI. ARITHMETIC.

The time wasted in acquiring four additional alphabets is partly compensated by the time saved in arithmetic through the Metric System. Would that England and America were willing to follow the example of other countries in this respect.

The method of teaching arithmetic is that used in our best schools, and known here as the Grube method.

Mental arithmetic is practiced much more than in New York.

VII. GEOGRAPHY.

Geography, as with us, begins in the third school year with a description of the school-house and the school district. It is taught in connection with history. The pupils learn thoroughly the geography of the mother and neighboring countries. Their ideas of other parts of the world, including America, are rather vague, as a rule.

VIII. HISTORY.

History is much better taught than in most of our schools. This is deemed necessary in order to develop a spirit of patriotism and loyalty to the Emperor. There is no subject in our public schools which is so imperfectly taught as United States history. It is high time to devote our attention to modern methods of teaching this most important branch of common school work.

IX. NATURAL HISTORY.

As will be seen by reference to courses of study, natural history, in its broadest sense, receives far more attention than in New York. This work seems rather difficult for elementary schools. In fact, the government has noted a tendency toward abstract and technical instruction, and directed the school commissioners and teachers to simplify the work. This subject is considered one of the most important in the elementary school *curriculum*. To be beneficial, however, it must be very simply taught.

X. MUSIC.

It is well known that the Germans, as a people, are far ahead of us in all that pertains to music, which is an essential factor in their elementary school course. It is to be hoped that we shall soon follow their example, at least as regards attention paid to memorizing national songs. These patriotic songs not only awaken love toward the Fatherland, but also, another most important feature, tend to lessen the influence of vulgar popular music. We are far from having so fine a collection as the Germans of national songs and songs of the people.

We have, however, much that is good, and more attention should be devoted to its memorization.

It is to be noted that the Germans follow, in teaching music in elementary schools, the old system of *solfeggio* or *Solmization*, as they call it. This system is now about 800 years old.

Although courses of study suggest that singing in unison is all that teachers may expect to accomplish, except under the most favorable circumstances, experience shows that these conditions exist very often. Visitors to Prussian elementary schools will hear frequently most excellent singing in several parts. In Prussia all male elementary school teachers must be able to play more or less upon the violin. Among them there is an astonishing number of thorough musicians.

XI. PHYSICAL TRAINING.

Prussian courses of study show that considerable attention is paid to physical training. Germany suffers from the lack of a national game corresponding to English cricket or American base ball. These games, with intervals of tennis, boating, swimming and other out-of-door sports, do more toward the physical development of English and American children than the detailed instructions of the Prussian educational department regulating physical exercises. The three years' military service of the Germans is, unquestionably, the most important factor in their physical development, as a people. This service begins at twenty years of age, and, up to this time, the youth is far from having that suppleness of body and quickness of action which characterize American young men.

In Prussia the object of physical training in the elementary schools is to insure strength to complete satisfactorily the amount of mental work laid down by law. Teachers are directed to watch carefully over the health of their pupils. Special attention is paid to proper carriage and postures, near-sightedness and deafness. It is the teacher's duty to give notice of blind and deaf and dumb pupils or those threatened with blindness and loss of hearing, that same may be sent to the institutions provided for such cases.

As regards the necessity in American elementary schools of apparatus for gymnastic exercises, such as parallel and horizontal bars, etc., it may be said generally that such apparatus is needed only in city schools where children have little opportunity for physical exercise.

XII. INDUSTRIAL TRAINING FOR GIRLS.

This course in Prussian elementary schools is practical, quite thorough and inexpensive. Its object is to fit girls for domestic life. Fancy stitching is not taught. Girls learn only plain household work.

A similar course should be introduced generally in New York elementary schools.

XIII. DRAWING.

Instruction in drawing in Prussian elementary schools now follows the method of Dr. A. Stuhlmann, introduced generally by the Prussian ministry in 1887 ("*Leitfaden für den Zeichenunterricht von Dr. A. Stuhlmann*"— *Spemann, Berlin, 1890*).

Dr. A. Stuhlmann makes three divisions of the work for elementary schools.

(1) Second and third school years: Drawing with the aid of squares (*Netzzeichnen*).

(2) Fourth, fifth and sixth school years: Free drawing of plane figures.

(3) Seventh and eighth school years: Free drawing from solid bodies.

A fourth course, also for the seventh and eighth school years, is devoted to work from plaster of Paris models.

Work in drawing is simple, systematic and thoroughly practical. It consists of the drawing of symmetrical figures, characteristic forms of plants, simple work in ornamental drawing, etc. Eye and hand are trained with especial reference to industrial drawing.

XIV. TRAINING OF CHILDREN IN THE LOVE OF THE FATHERLAND.

In Prussian schools the utmost pains are taken to foster the spirit of patriotism. The law requires that a likeness of the Emperor be placed in each school-room. Courses of study improve every opportunity to call attention to the importance of cultivating a national spirit. From the cradle, the Prussian child learns the national songs. At every step one is reminded that Prussia is a land of patriots.

In New York the appointment of Arbor Day was the first movement toward the recognition of the importance of this subject in connection with our schools. This attempt to cultivate a national spirit is most praiseworthy. Teachers and all school officers should spare no pains in developing a proper spirit of patriotism and love of our free institutions. If this were done as in Prussia, the history and geography of our own country would no longer be looked upon by pupils as dry and uninteresting.

XV. TEXT-BOOKS.

A complete list is made by the government of all text-books which may be used in the schools. This list must be followed. The director of a high school and the school commissioner in the case of an elementary school, are forced, if they desire to introduce a new book, to state the defects of the old one and the advantages of the proposed substitute and submit this statement, with a copy of the new book, to the government. There is but one time of the year in which new books may be introduced.

Prussian elementary schools use fewer text-books for pupils and more reference books for teachers than New York elementary schools.

The paper, binding and printing of our school-books is much better than that of the German books. Our books present a much more attractive appearance, but are more expensive in consequence. German text-books are often mere outlines. The first book in geography covers only the government district. Each government district uses a special book for this purpose. This peculiarity is worth of note. Another peculiarity is the text-book in the *Realien*, embracing geography, history and natural history. The readers offer at times an illustration of the danger of pushing too far a principle good *per se*. This principle is to take up only the work of standard authors. Statistics and descriptions of America and rapidly growing cities and countries in other parts of the world, written years ago, do not give as a rule a very correct idea of the state of things to-day. Readers in present use in Prussian elementary schools contain examples establishing the justice of this criticism.

All pupils must be supplied with books. In the school lists of pupils, the occupation of the father is always given, and it is the duty of the teacher to know what children must be supplied with books. Except in the case of poverty, when books and stationery are furnished free of charge, parents and guardians can be forced by law to provide them. This happens, indeed, very seldom.

As is the case where teachers are properly trained, Prussian instructors use text-books very little in recitations. I have often been present for hours at recitations in elementary schools when the teacher did not refer a single time to a text or reference book.

Text-books are free only to the children of indigent parents. They are not printed by the government. In drawing up the official lists of text-books which may be used, care is taken to avoid an unnecessary variety. The State aims to insure uniformity in each province in the text-books used in all schools of the same class.

XVI. APPARATUS USED IN TEACHING.

Except in the case of blackboard surface, which, according to our standard, is inferior in quality and entirely inadequate in extent, Prussian elementary schools are generally far better supplied than our own with apparatus used in teaching. As will be seen from the regulations under courses of study, the government fixes definitely the *minimum* of articles required in teaching in each class. It is the exception when schools are not far more fully furnished with such apparatus than the letter of the law requires.

XVII. TEACHERS' LIBRARIES.

These libraries are under the charge of the school commissioner and a committee of his teachers. They are composed of works on pedagogics, history, natural history, school journals and reading matter of general interest to teachers. In connection therewith, one often finds very good collections of minerals, bugs, etc. These libraries are supported by and accessible to the teachers of the school-commissioner district. For a very small sum, say twenty-five cents a year, teachers have the use of books which they could not afford to buy. The regulations for these libraries, which are set up in the place of residence of the school commissioner, are very like those of our New York loaning libraries.

XVIII. INTEREST OF THE GENERAL PUBLIC IN SCHOOL WORK.

This is in striking contrast with the indifference of the people of New York. Parks and skating-rinks, botanical and zoölogical gardens, gymnasia and swimming schools, libraries and museums are opened to the school children. Teachers attend with their classes special theatrical performances of German and foreign classics.

THIRD CHAPTER.

Religious Instruction.

Religious instruction is the foundation-stone of elementary school work in Prussia. This instruction, both in the public and in the private schools, is compulsory. It is regulated by law, is entirely impartial, and is considered an essential part of the education of each pupil. Roman Catholics, Protestants and Jews have masters of their own faith, but no one can give religious instruction who is not authorized by the general government. Except in the country, all elementary schools are confessional. In the case of these rural mixed schools, the religious belief of the teacher depends on that of a plurality of the pupils. To entitle children to special religious instruction other than that of a plurality of the pupils, there must be at least twelve pupils who demand it. When possible, it is desirable that schools unite for this purpose.

In the maintenance of local schools, Jews and Christians have the same legal rights. In Jewish secondary schools, Christian teachers are sometimes employed, but not *vice versa*. Indeed, with the exception of schools of art, of industry and of navigation, the Jews can teach only in Jewish schools. Every synagogue community is forced by law to give the necessary instruction in Judaism to children between the ages of 6 and 14. It may be said briefly that pupils must receive instruction in accordance with the religious belief of their parents. Unbaptized children of Roman Catholics or Protestants receive naturally religious instruction in accordance with the faith of their parents. A teacher can not force a pupil to receive other religious instruction than that in the faith of his parents, except at the request of these parents.

It must not be overlooked that Prussian parents can choose for their children a public school, a private school or instruction in the family. All private schools, however, are under the immediate supervision of the government, and teachers in these private schools must have the same qualifications as the teachers in the public schools. Furthermore, if instruction be given in the family, the government has the duty, through her supervising officers, to see that said instruction be an equivalent for that given in the public schools. Inasmuch as religious instruction is an essential part of the elementary school *curriculum*, the teachers must be qualified. The time-tables under Courses of Study, given in the sixth chapter, show how regular this religious instruction is, both for Roman Catholics and for Protestants.

In connection with religious instruction, it should be stated that clergymen in Prussia, are to a certain extent officers of the State. A majority receive a part of their salary, sometimes half, directly from the State treasury. They must all have absolved the gymnasial course of nine years and the university course of three or four years or a theological course in a divinity school of recognized standing.

The following is a brief summary of the principal decrees regulating religious instruction:

(1) Decision as to the character of religious instruction depends principally upon the father.

(2) It is the father's duty to see that the child receive religious instruction conformable to his faith and condition in life.
(3) Children born in wedlock must receive instruction in the religion of the father.
(4) No legal contracts can be made to change the rule *sub* 3.
(5) In the case of mixed marriages, agreements made before or at marriage to train the children in the religion of the mother have no legal force.
(6) If father and mother, however, agree as to the religious instruction their children are to receive, no third person has authority to interfere.
(7) At the death of the father, the religious instruction in his faith must be continued.
(8) No attention is to be paid to death-bed conversions to another faith.
(9) If, however, the child has received, the last entire year before death of father, religious instruction according to the mother's faith, this instruction must be continued until the said child be 14 years of age.
(10) After the death of the father, it becomes the duty of the court for guardianship (*Vormundschaftsgericht*) to see that the child receive religious instruction according to law.
(11) Children born out of wedlock receive, until 14 years of age, religious instruction according to the faith of the mother.
(12) They who assume care of a child abandoned by his parents acquire the rights of parents, and therefore, decide as to the character of religious instruction until said child be 14 years of age.
(13) The same rule holds good in the case of adopted children.
(14) When 14 years of age, children can decide for themselves as to the religious denomination to which they will belong.
(15) Before 14 years of age, no religious denomination can receive a child or permit an open confession of faith other than that to which said child belongs by law.

DIVISION OF CHILDREN OF SCHOOL AGE IN THE PUBLIC ELEMENTARY SCHOOLS ACCORDING TO RELIGIOUS FAITH UPON MAY 20, 1886.

The hours devoted to religious instruction vary from four to six weekly.

	Teachers.	Pupils.
23,122 Protestant schools with	*41,539	‖2,993,852
10,061 Roman Catholic schools with	†19,632	‖1,613,497
12 other Christian schools with	‡31	870
318 Jewish schools with	407	13,270
503 mixed § schools with	3,141	216,758
34,016	64,750	4,838,247

* Including three of other Christian bodies.
† Including one Protestant.
‡ Including three Protestants.
§ In 318 of these mixed schools for Romanists and Protestants, there are special religious teachers.
‖ 54,960 Roman Catholic pupils attended Protestant schools and 25,878 Protestant pupils, Roman Catholic schools.

FOURTH CHAPTER.

SCHOOL-HOUSES AND SITES.

Prussia labors under the disadvantage of having many school-houses which were built before much attention was paid to heating, lighting, ventilation and other sanitary arrangements. As regards school-desks, she is still very conservative. Many new elementary schools which are looked upon as models are furnished with the old desk, five and six pupils to each desk. In fact, the normal Prussian elementary school-room has but two rows of desks, one on either side, with a broad aisle in the center. Pupils near the wall, to pass out, must walk along the seat, the others leaning forward to give them a foothold.

The regulations touching school buildings are quite detailed, but, as is too often the case with us, are not always strictly enforced. These regulations, stated briefly, are as follows (Düsseldorf):

1. *School-house site.* This must be in a sunny and dry open space, remote from the most frequented streets, and from everything likely to disturb the instruction or injurious to the health of the pupils. In large districts care should be taken to choose a site near the center. Good drinking-water must be furnished. The site should be large enough to afford the necessary play-ground. If possible, the building should stand entirely free from other buildings. When necessary to build near the street, an open space should be left, that the children, in leaving the school, step not directly into the street.

2. *School-rooms.* When possible, these are to be upon the ground floor. If more than one story be necessary, the younger pupils should have the ground floor. Where special class-rooms are provided for boys and girls, they should be furnished with separate entrances.

If teacher is to reside in school-house, his apartment should be separated from the school-rooms, and, if possible, should have a private entrance. In building a school-house, care should be taken for additions which may be necessary in the future.

3. *Construction of building.* Stone or brick is the rule. Frame buildings can be built only when special local conditions make it advisable. All walls must be isolated by asphalt, glass or cement, below the ground floor and above the ground level. The roofs are to be covered with a fire-proof material. The eaves are to be provided with gutters and conductors. The floor of the school-room must be at least one-half meter above the ground, and when there is no cellar, care should be taken that same be perfectly dry. The partitions between floors should be packed, to insure quiet. Columns to support ceilings or roof should not be placed within the school-rooms. Around the building there should be a gutter, at least one meter wide, provided with conductor to carry off the water.

4. *Use of building after completion.* The new building is not to be used until thoroughly dry. In the case of buildings of brick and stone, this will not be within less than six months after the completion of the walls.

5. *Size of the school-rooms.* This depends upon the number of pupils. School-rooms for more than eighty pupils are not allowed. For every child there must be a floor space of at least three-quarters of a square

meter, in which the necessary room for passages, desks and stoves is included. A class-room for eighty children demands, therefore, a space of sixty square meters. School-rooms for less than fifty pupils must be large enough to afford floor space for each child of at least one square meter. The length of school-room should be to the breadth as three to two; only in the case of classes for less than fifty pupils is the form approaching the square permissible. The length of the room from the last desk to the blackboard should not exceed nine meters. Where school-rooms are lighted from but one side, the distance from the farthest desk to the nearest window should not exceed six meters. Ceilings under four meters are not allowed. Floor space and height must be so measured that each child, by natural ventilation, have not less than three cubic meters' space.

6. *The floor* of the school-room must be level and solid. It is advisable to oil the same.

7. *The walls* and ceiling must be smooth. The walls should be painted light blue or green (one poisonless color); the ceilings whitewashed or calcimined.

8. *The doors* must be at least a meter wide, and must open outwardly. The children should face the entrance.

9. *The windows.* Care should be taken to prevent, during school hours, direct or reflected sunlight. Where this is not possible, windows should be supplied with curtains. *Marquisen*, that is, curtains of slats of wood, are especially good, in that they do not interfere with the ventilation. Curtains of dark green are best. The light should come to the pupil over the left shoulder from behind; windows facing the children are not allowed, and, only in exceptional cases, windows on both sides. The school-room is the better lighted in proportion to the height of the light above the floor. The area of the window openings must, where school building is in an open space, be at least one-fifth that of the floor space. This is to be increased where light is shut off by other buildings, trees, etc. The space between two windows along the wall should not exceed one meter and a quarter. All windows must be made to open easily.

10. *Heating.* The stoves should be so placed as to afford, so far as possible, the same temperature throughout the school-room. They should not be placed, as a rule, in the center of the school-room. The best place is generally near the long wall free from windows. They should be provided with a screen of sheet-iron or tin. Dampers in stove-pipe should never be made to close tightly. In large school buildings, central heating is recommended. To insure the proper temperature, thirteen to sixteen degrees R. (sixty-one and one-quarter degrees to sixty-eight degrees F.), a thermometer must be placed in every school-room, at least one meter and a half above the floor, and at a point where the mean temperature may be ascertained.*

11. *Ventilation.* Every school-room must be properly ventilated. Inasmuch as, during school-hours, windows should not be opened wide, the upper sashes should be made to open outwardly on a pivot.

* In elementary schools in Prussia, when thermometer registers above twenty-two degrees R. (eighty-one and five-tenths degrees F.) in the shade at 11 A. M., there is generally no afternoon session. In higher schools, this matter is in the discretion of the director.

In the opposite walls ventilators should be placed at about the same height. Care should be taken in heating that foul air be removed and fresh air introduced. The first is to be accomplished by ventilation-pipes connected with the chimney; the latter by a cold-air box under the floor, introducing cold air into the open space between the stove and covering. Where central heating is used there must be an approved system of ventilation.

12. *Halls and stairs.* These must be light, roomy and free from draughts. The main halls should not be less than two and one-half meters wide. All stairs must be convenient, never too steep. Steps before the entrance should be of stone and provided with railings. Stairways should be at least one and a quarter meters wide. The height of the steps should not exceed nineteen centimeters. Winding stairs are not allowed, nor should single flights from story to story be built without landings. The open side of stairways is to be provided with a balustrade, the other side with hand railings. In large school buildings the stairs should be of brick, iron or stone. Foot mats should be placed at the foot of each flight of stairs.

13. *Dwelling of teacher.* If in school building and for a married teacher, this must consist of five living rooms, and in addition, a kitchen, pantry, cellar and garret. For an unmarried teacher, one living and one sleeping room. For a female teacher, a kitchen, cellar and garret are also necessary. When there are several teachers' apartments in the same building, these should be properly separated. If the size of site permit, space should be given to teacher for a garden. This space must not be taken from the play-ground.

14. *Privies.* These should be without the school buildings, with separate accommodations for the sexes. They should be so placed that the prevalent winds blow not toward the school building. For eighty boys there should be at least two separate privies, for eighty girls at least three. The doors should be provided with bolts from within. Each compartment should not be less than three-quarters of a meter wide and one and one-quarter meters deep. The height of the seats, according to the age of the children, varies from thirty-five-one-hundredths to forty-five-one-hundredths of a meter. These seats must be provided with covers. The pits must be water-tight and provided with ventilating-pipes. Urinals must be provided for the boys, separated by partitions of sufficient height to leave the shoulders alone visible.

15. *Play-ground.* This should be as near as convenient to the school-house, so that, if possible, the whole may be overlooked from the school building. Each pupil must have at least two and one-half square meters space. The whole must be properly drained. The borders may be planted with trees. Each play-ground must be provided with the necessary apparatus for gymnastic exercises, and, according to need, benches. When possible, a part of the play-ground should be covered for use in rainy weather.

16. *School-desks.* These must be made with special regard to the health of the pupils. All must be provided with backs. The general rule is to bind together desk and seat so that each pupil have a space from fifty-one-hundredths to sixty-one-hundredths of a meter. Desks should be regulated in size according to the age of the children.

Desks for two pupils are recommended. Plans for the ordinary desks (for from four to six pupils) are furnished.
17. *Position of desks.* The desks should be so placed that the light falls over the left shoulder of the children. In the rear and upon the long window-side, there should be a free space of at least four meters; in front, a free space of at least two and a half meters.
18. *The teacher's desk.* This should be placed upon a platform two and one-half meters deep, one and one-fourth meters wide, fifteen-one-hundredths meters high.
19. *Blackboards, etc.* Each school-room must be provided with the necessary number of blackboards and a closet for the preservation of the objects used in teaching.
20. *When no cloak-room exists,* pegs for overcoats and hats should be placed in the school-room.
21. *New school buildings.* When, in the judgment of the *Local* and *Kreisschulinspektor,* with the concurrence of the *Landrath* and district architect, the building of a new school is deemed necessary, the district architect must submit to the government a plan with an estimate of cost. If the plan be accepted, the district builder advertises for bids for the necessary building material. The best and cheapest is taken and the district builder, who is personally responsible, goes on with the building. The wisdom of this provision is seen from the fact that such buildings never exceed the estimates, while in the case of buildings not under governmental control, the cost is often fifty per cent greater than the original estimate.

OBSERVATIONS.

New York has little to learn from Prussia as regards school buildings. Regulations are often transgressed there as here. School-rooms, as I saw, are frequently overcrowded.
The ministerial decree of March 26, 1827, fixes a limit of eighty pupils for ungraded schools and seventy for each class in graded schools. In 1886, only 53.84 per cent of all the children received instruction under these conditions.
May 5, 1873, the minister of public instruction was forced to decree that the following state of things was to be tolerated for the time being.

Under one teacher................................. From 80 to 120
Under two teachers................................ From 120 to 200
Under three teachers.............................. From 200 to 300

But even these limits are often exceeded in districts where the population is rapidly increasing.
In Posen the average number of children falling to one teacher in 1886, was seventy-four in the city schools and 110 in the country schools. In fifteen of the thirty-six government districts (*Regierungsbezirke*), the average number of children, falling to one teacher, exceeded eighty in the country, and in three government districts in the city schools. In the whole kingdom there were 23,152 schools with one teacher, 6,592 of which were overcrowded. It is worthy of note that only 8,826 pupils were not received directly because of insufficient school accommodations.

Official statistics show that there were only 4,012 classes with less than 30 pupils, 1,995 of which were in ungraded schools.

With 4,838,247 pupils in her public elementary schools, Prussia employed, in 1886, 64,750 regular teachers. In New York public schools in 1886, 31,325* teachers were employed and the total number of children in attendance at any time during the year was only 1,027,767. In other words, the average number falling to one teacher in Prussia was a fraction above 74; in New York, a fraction above 32.

These figures show the great disadvantage under which we are placed by the very unequal distribution of our population. When we add to this, our most unjust system of local taxation for school purposes, it seems astonishing that small rural districts maintain the schools as they are at present. It is not surprising that all who have given the subject thought are practically unanimous in favor of the township system.

School-rooms in Prussia are often dark and poorly ventilated. Privies are frequently in the same buildings, and in mixed rural schools, proper provision is not always made for separate accommodations for the sexes.

In the erection of new buildings, the regulations are strictly enforced and class-rooms are not built to accommodate more than eighty pupils.

Of the total number of pupils in attendance upon the public elementary schools May 20, 1886, 4,706,300 were within less than two miles of the schools attended, 131,947 were at a greater distance.

FIFTH CHAPTER.

I. INSTITUTIONS FOR CHILDREN UNDER SCHOOL AGE.

Although somewhat foreign to the subject in hand, before considering the elementary schools proper, reference is made to the different institutions for children under school age.

1. *Krippen* (*Crèches*).

These are upon the plan first introduced at Paris, by Marbeau, in 1844. Babies, whose mothers are forced to work for a living, are kept until 2 years of age. They are cared for in these institutions upon working days, the mothers calling for them every evening.

2. *Kinderbewahranstalten*.

These are for the children of the laboring classes until 4 years of age. They were first introduced into Germany in 1802. Young children receive the care which parents are unable to give them at home.

3. *Kleinkinderschulen*.

These continue to care for the children of the poorer classes until they become of school age. France founded these institutions in 1801. They were soon adopted in Germany.

---

*Only 22,240 were employed for a continuous term of twenty-eight weeks or more.

4. *Kindergärten.*

These were intended originally for the children of the wealthier classes under school age. The first Kindergarten was founded by Froebel in 1840. In 1851 they were proscribed by the governments of Prussia and Saxony, upon the ground that they planted the seeds of socialism and atheism. Kindergärten were then forced to abandon the theories and organization of Froebel, and most of them adopted the name of play-schools (*Spielschulen*).

The fundamental ideas of Froebel were better understood somewhat later, and the ban placed upon Kindergärten was raised.

For some years past enthusiasts have urged, without success, the advisability of making Kindergärten public.

The institutions for children under school age were founded, for the most part, by private individuals and charitable societies. Generally speaking, the Germans recognize alone the advantages of institutions of the first three classes where, strictly speaking, no attempt is made to teach the children. In manufacturing districts, where parents can not look at all after their children during the day, such institutions are considered matters of necessity. City governments sometimes maintain these institutions.

Ministerial decrees refer to all institutions for children under school age as *Kinderbewahranstalten*, *Warteschulen* and *Kindergärten*. The names under 2, 3 and 4 are often used interchangeably. They are controlled by the State in the same manner as other private institutions and are found, as a rule, only in larger cities.

As regards the last three classes of these institutions, *Kinderbewahranstalten*, *Kleinkinderschulen* and *Kindergärten*, the government instructions to school commissioners are very strict. They must see that rooms be of sufficient size to accommodate the children enrolled; that same be properly ventilated, heated and lighted; and that the persons in charge do not encroach in the least upon elementary school work.

In some provinces considerable trouble has been occasioned by the fact that children have been kept in these institutions until 9 or 10 years of age. The following provisions for Schleswig-Holstein, from May 31, 1884, will serve to show how this matter has been regulated.

a. Private institutions for children, both under and of school age, should not be authorized except under very exceptional local conditions.

b. The time children are to attend such institutions, when authorized, must be definitely stated and is not to exceed the eighth year of age.

c. Children of school age must receive distinct elementary instruction in a separate school-room.

d. These conditions apply to all present existing institutions. If the condition *sub* (*c.*) can not be carried out, children of school age must leave said institutions at Easter next year.*

II. THE VARIOUS INSTITUTIONS FOR CHILDREN OF SCHOOL AGE.

The Prussian child between the ages of 6 and 14 may be in attendance upon any one of the following institutions:

---
* There is generally but one time of year, and that Easter, for admission of children into the elementary schools.

1. The different *Gymnasia:* The full course at these high schools lasts nine years, and begins after three years of primary instruction.
2. The *Mittelschulen:* There is really no gradation between elementary and middle schools. The latter merely go on somewhat further with elementary school work, introducing French, Latin and English. The advanced class in an elementary school of six classes may be permitted to follow the course of study for middle schools.
3. Institutions for the blind (*Blindenanstalten*).
4. Deaf and dumb asyla (*Taubstummen-Bildungsanstalten*).
5. Orphan asyla (*Waisenanstalten*).
6. Insane asyla (*Idiotenanstalten*).
7. Reform schools (*Rettungsanstalten*).
8. The elementary schools proper (*Elementarschulen*).

He may receive instruction in a public school, a private school or in the family. There are very few private schools in Prussia, however, and all are under the immediate supervision of the government. As a rule, private schools may be founded only where there is a lack of public school accommodations. Teachers in these private schools must have the same qualifications as those required by law for the public schools. In case of children instructed at home, the government school inspectors are authorized to test the qualifications of the persons who give said instruction. They can demand, furthermore, courses and hours of study to see that instruction given at home be an equivalent to the instruction given in the public schools.

Of the high schools, the most important are *Gymnasien* and *Realgymnasien.* As is seen by the following list of studies * and weekly divisions of time, the former devote a great deal of attention to the classics, the latter to modern languages, natural sciences and mathematics. As a rule, children must have attained the age of 9 before admission to *Serta*, the lowest class in *Gymnasien* and *Realschulen.*

GYMNASIEN.

	I.	II.	III.	IV.	V.	VI.	VII.	VIII.	IX.
Religion		2	2	2	2	2	2	2	2
Language (German)	4	2	2	2	2	2	2	3	3
Latin	9	9	9	9	9	8	8	8	8
Greek					7	7	7	6	6
French		4	5	2	2	2	2	2	2
History and geography	3	3	1	2	3	3	3	3	3
Mathematics	1	4	4	3	4	4	4	4	4
Natural history	2	2	2	2	2				
Physics						2	2	2	2
Penmanship	2	2							
Drawing	2	2	2						
Gymnastics	2	2	2	2	2	2	2	2	2
Music (vocal)	2	2	2	2	2	2	2	2	2
	32	34	34	34	34	34	34	34	34

* As given in the report of the Massachusetts Board of Education in 1890.

REALGYMNASIEN.

	I.	II.	III.	IV.	V.	VI.	VII.	VIII.	IX.
Religion	3	2	2	2	2	2	2	2	2
Language (German)	3	3	3	3	3	3	3	3	3
Latin	8	7	7	6	6	5	5	5	5
French	....	5	5	4	4	4	4	4	4
English	....	....	....	4	4	3	3	3	3
History and geography	3	3	4	4	4	3	3	3	3
Natural history	2	2	2	2	2	2	....	....	....
Physics	....	....	....	....	....	3	3	3	3
Chemistry	....	....	....	....	....	....	2	2	2
Mathematics	5	4	5	5	5	5	5	5	5
Penmanship	3	2	....	....	....	....	....	....	....
Drawing	2	2	2	2	2	2	2	2	2
	29	30	30	32	32	32	32	32	32

Instruction in gymnastics and singing is given partly or entirely outside of these hours.

In 1886 there were 576 public middle schools in Prussia with an attendance of 134,937 pupils.* The following is a list of the subjects studied with weekly division of time (*"Preussische Statistik 101"*):

	I.	II.	III.	IV.	V.	VI.
Religion	2	2	2	3	3	3
Language (German)	4	6	8	12	12	12
Arithmetic	3	3	3	5	5	5
Geometry	3	2	2	....	....	....
Natural history	2	2	2	....	....	....
Physics (chemistry)	3	2	....	....	....	....
Geography	2	2	2	2	....	....
History	2	2	2	....	....	....
French	5	5	5	....	....	....
Drawing	2	2	2	2	....	....
Music	2	2	2	2	2	2
Gymnastics	2	2	2	2	2	2
	32	32	32	28	24	24

There is at least one institution for the blind (*Blindenanstalt*) in each province except Hohenzollern. In Westphalia and Hessen-Nassau there are two. The majority are public institutions. There are sufficient accommodations for the blind of school age for the whole kingdom. In 1886, there were 532 children of school age in these asyla.

In 1886, there were thirty-one insane asyla in Prussia, which cared for 1,521 children of school age. In the 170 elementary schools connected with orphan asyla and houses of correction, 10,119 children of school age received instruction in 1886. Insane asyla, orphan asyla and houses of correction are not, for the most part, public institutions. They come under the jurisdiction of the Minister of Public Instruction only in a restricted sense. As a rule, special schools are connected with houses of correction only. Orphans attend generally the regular elementary schools.

* Including also the public secondary schools for girls. In 1886, the number of boys in all middle and high schools was 217,190. The number of girls in all secondary schools was 137,661. The course of study in secondary schools for girls is from two to three years shorter than in the corresponding schools for boys. Many girls are educated in foreign countries. Statistics do not include these girls.
Drs. Schneider and Petersilie reckon that 207,000 boys as against 155,000 girls receive a secondary education.

Since 1788, forty-eight asyla for the deaf and dumb have been founded. Thirty-eight of these institutions are public and seven are maintained by large societies. In 1886, there were 3,913 children of school age in attendance. The deaf and dumb of school age are forced to attend these institutions only in the province of Schleswig-Holstein.

May 20, 1886, 4,848,247 pupils of school age were in attendance upon the public elementary schools, and there were only 249,280 pupils of school age in all other schools, public and private, which receive children of school age.

It is my aim to dwell only upon the normal divisions of Prussian elementary schools proper, for in these schools the great mass of the children of school age receive instruction. We shall, then, have a clear idea of the *minimum* of work required of each healthy child under normal conditions.

SIXTH CHAPTER.

COURSES OF STUDY IN PRUSSIAN ELEMENTARY SCHOOLS.

The normal divisions of Prussian elementary schools are as follows:

1. *The school with one teacher.* This is either the (a) *Einklassige Volksschule* (ungraded school) or (b) the *Halbtagsschule* (half-day school).

(a) *Einklassige Volksschule.* All children of school age receive instruction in the same school-room from the same teacher. The number of pupils should not exceed eighty.

The children of the lowest class have in the rule twenty hours per week; those of the middle and upper classes thirty hours, including gymnastic exercises for the boys and the manual training for the girls.

(b) *Halbtagsschule.* When the number of pupils exceeds eighty, or the school-room is too small to accommodate even this number, and conditions are not favorable for the appointment of a second teacher, with permission of the government, a *Halbtagsschule* (half-day school) may be organized, whose classes together have weekly thirty-two hours instruction.

2. *The school with two teachers.* Instruction must be given in separate classes. If the number of the pupils exceeds 120, a third class is to be formed. In this school, with three classes and two teachers, the third class receives twelve hours of instruction weekly, the second class twenty-four and the third class twenty-eight.

3. *The school with three teachers.* In schools of three classes, the children of the lowest class receive weekly twenty-two hours of instruction; those of the middle class twenty-eight; those of the upper class thirty-two.

4. *Schools with four or more teachers.* The pupils of the lowest classes receive weekly twenty-two hours of instruction, those of the middle classes twenty-eight, those of the upper classes thirty-two.

In schools with three or more teachers, division of the sexes is desirable in the upper classes. In a school with two teachers, the organization of two or three classes is preferable to that of two ungraded schools where the sexes are divided.

Where several ungraded schools exist in one locality, it is desirable to form a graded school.

All schools must submit annually, before the beginning of the school year, a course of study to the supervising officers. The elementary schools submit their courses of study to the school commissioners (*Kreisschulinspektoren*) and local inspectors (*Lokalschulinspektoren*), the higher schools to the provincial school consistory (*Provinzial-Schulcollegium*). The work to be accomplished is defined by ministerial decrees. This work is here outlined as briefly as possible. Slight variations exist in different government districts and modifications are made to meet local needs.

I. COURSE OF STUDY FOR UNGRADED SCHOOLS.

Einklassige Volksschulen.

1. The lowest class has twenty hours of instruction weekly, the middle class also twenty, the upper class thirty. This time is divided as follows:*

	Lowest Class.	Middle Class.	Advanced Class.
a. Religious instruction	4	5	5
b. Language	11	10	8
c. Arithmetic	1	4	4
d. Geometry		0	1
e. Drawing	0	1	2
f. Realien (geography, history and natural history)	0	6	6
g. Music	1	2	2
h. Gymnastics (manual training)	0	2	2
	20	30	30

For division according to the days of the week, consult time-tables following the course of study.

Modifications of these time-tables may be authorized by the local school inspector, if they do not affect the total number of hours of instruction. Other modifications must be authorized by the government.

2. There should be three divisions of the pupils. The children of the lowest division, upon first entering school, must receive six months' practice in reading and writing the German script.

The lowest class embraces the two first years, the middle class the three following, the highest class the remaining years.

Reading forms the basis of gradation. The lowest class embraces the children who have the *Fibel* or primer and are learning to read; the second class those who are farther advanced but read with some difficulty; the first class those who read logically and with facility.

3. All schools must be supplied with the following: First, a copy of every text and reference book used in the school; second, a globe; third, a wall-map of the home province; fourth, a wall-map of Germany; fifth, a wall-map of Palestine; sixth, plates for instruction in natural history and philosophy; seventh, large alphabets of wood or

---

* The time pupils may work outside of school-hours is limited to one hour daily for the lowest class, one hour and one half for the middle class, and two hours for the advanced class.

of paste-board; eighth, a violin; ninth, a rule and a pair of compasses; tenth, a numerical frame; eleventh, bodies for teaching geometry; twelfth, two large blackboards; thirteenth, for Protestant schools, a Bible and a copy of the song-book used in the district.

In addition to the above, a thermometer, a likeness of the emperor, and, in Roman Catholic schools, a crucifix.

4. Records. The teacher must keep a school-register, showing the daily attendance and weekly progress of the pupils. He must also keep a history of his school-district.* The course of study and time-table must always be in the school-room.

5. Text-books, etc. First, the primer and readers; second, the primary arithmetic; third, the song-book; fourth, books for religious instruction; fifth, a slate, pencil, sponge, rule and compass; sixth, a diary; seventh, a copy-book.

Syllabus of work.

Introductory remark: Teachers should carefully prepare themselves for all lessons, the younger teachers especially with pen in hand. All work of pupils should be most conscientiously controlled.

a RELIGIOUS INSTRUCTION (not given).

b. LANGUAGE WORK (GERMAN). The pupils should be taught to speak and write correctly. Special attention should be given to letters and common business forms. A taste for good reading should be cultivated.

Lowest Division (eleven hours). Object teaching. Pupils are led to talk about objects which are brought to their notice. The teacher is to correct, carefully, faulty enunciation and incorrect expression. Instruction in reading and writing should follow the system taught in the normal school of the district. The alphabet method is absolutely forbidden. After six months' instruction pupils should be able to divide simple statements into words, the words into syllables, and the syllables into their respective sounds. They must be able to make and read each letter according to its sound.

At the close of six months the children are made acquainted with the printed characters and the names of the letters.

When children learn to read, they should be taught to associate words, and then statements, with the objects or idea represented, to prevent thoughtless, mechanical reading.

The pieces read should be thoroughly understood by the pupils. The principal thoughts are best brought out by questions on the part of the teacher.

In addition to short proverbs, aphorisms, etc., the pupils should learn by heart some short selections from the primer. They should also have practice in repeating, in their own words, what they have read.

The children of this division learn also the Roman printed characters.

In teaching writing, the teacher explains the formation of the letters upon the blackboard.

Before leaving this third and lowest division, the pupils should be able to read with facility, correct enunciation and expression the selections they have had. They should be able to answer questions as to what they have read; reproduce all selections in their own words, and copy correctly from the primer. They should also have had some exercise in writing at dictation.

Middle Class (ten hours). Further practice in reading, with more careful attention to subject-matter and expression.

Writing must now be taken up at fixed hours, the pupils using partly pen and ink.

Pupils are now to learn the formation of the plural of nouns. Statements are made embracing nouns in the singular and plural numbers. Pupils learn to recognize and employ in statements verbs and adjectives. Next come the declensions of nouns, with the definite and indefinite articles, the comparison of adjectives, tenses and modes of verbs. All this work is taken up very simply and only through many practical examples. Pupils are taught to transpose simple sentences, and to recognize the principal parts of simple sentences.

The pupils are now ready for simple work in composition. The teacher chooses a subject, generally connected with school work, writes a short outline upon the blackboard, and the pupils complete the same, first orally and then in writing.

Before promotion to the advanced class, pupils should be able to repeat, in their own words, the substance of the selections they have read; to read the same with facility, both in the German and Roman characters, to write correctly a simple exercise at dictation, and to reproduce in writing, in their own words, any simple selection which has been taken up in the class.

Advanced Class (eight hours). In reading, about thirty selections annually are studied so carefully that the children understand well both form and subject-matter. Pupils should be taught to reproduce selections read in correct and logical order.

A number of poems, particularly *Volkslieder*, songs of the people, should be learned by heart, and repeated until fixed in memory.

---

* The reports of the ministry show that these histories often prove valuable in recording discoveries of antiquities, heathen burial-places, etc.

Before leaving the school, all pupils should be able to read readily and understandingly even difficult articles which, in subject-matter, are not too foreign to their line of vision.

Orthography and punctuation are taught by repeated and constant practice in reading, dictation and composition. Should special faults often occur, the teacher learns thereby to what he should devote most particularly the attention of the class.

It is necessary to drill the pupils repeatedly upon words alike in form and sound, and upon the most common foreign words used in German. This is best done by the composition of sentences, showing at the same time both the meaning and the orthography of the words in question.

Fixed hours are appointed for the perfection of the pupils in the German and Latin script. It is advisable to select for this purpose proverbs of the people, and ordinary business forms.

Pupils must learn to write neatly, legibly and in good form. Pains must be taken with all written work.

The different forms of sentences are taught, with special regard to punctuation. Pupils are drilled on parts of speech and in the analysis of sentences.

Examples are taken, so far as possible, from selections the pupils have read.

Composition, as in the middle class, is continued by exercises in reproduction. Subjects are chosen connected with the *curriculum*.

The pupils are often asked to write, at the close of a lesson, what has been learned in geography, natural history, history of the Fatherland, etc.

Written solutions of problems in arithmetic are often required. Letters must be prepared ready to post. Repeated drill upon ordinary business forms, receipts, notes. etc., is ordered.

Before graduation, pupils have considerable practice in original composition.

c. ARITHMETIC. The pupils should acquire a thorough knowledge of practical business arithmetic. They must be trained to give reasons for steps in the solution of problems. Mechanical work must be avoided. Pupils should be most carefully drilled in the system of coinage, weights and measures of the mother country. Problems should be practical. The teacher should avoid long rows of figures, beyond the comprehension of the pupils, and take up only that which will be of use to them in trade or in every-day life.

In introducing a new process, in all classes mental should precede written work.

Lowest Class (four hours). The figures from one to ten, use of objects, marks, points, crosses, etc. The numerical frame. The four fundamental processes from one to ten. Gradually extended to 100. A great variety of simple problems embracing the numbers from one to 100.

Middle Class (four hours). The figures up to 1000. The four processes are exercised by problems in mental arithmetic up to 1000, especially, however, up to 200. The pupils learn system of coinage, weights and measures. Practice in written work beyond the number 1000.

Advanced Class (four hours). Common and decimal fractions. In common fractions, children should be drilled particularly in those which come up in every day life (one-half to one-twelfth). Special care should be taken in teaching the reduction of common to decimal fractions, and this method of solution of problems involving unusual common fractions is recommended. Computations of time, ratio and proportion, percentage, interest, profit and loss, discount, partnership, alligation, area of surfaces and contents of solids.

d. GEOMETRY - *Advanced Class (one hour)*. This instruction should be connected with drawing on the one hand and arithmetic on the other. By the former, pupils learn to represent correctly lines, surfaces and solids; by the latter, they understand how to compute the length of lines, the area of surfaces and the contents of solids.

This instruction should be practical, tending to meet the needs of tradesmen and farmers. It should be given in a simple manner.

The course includes lines, angles, triangles, quadrilaterals, polygons, circles and the regular solid bodies.

e. DRAWING.* Training of the eye and of the hand, is the object of the course in drawing. A taste for symmetry, regularity and beauty of form should be developed. Instruction should be practical, the aim being to afford assistance to those especially who will learn a trade.

Middle Class (one hour). Drawing begins in the middle class, and consists entirely of mechanical work, with the slate, rule and pencil, in copying lines and figures placed upon the blackboard by the teacher.

Advanced Class (two hours). This work is continued with paper and pencil. The pupils now begin free-hand drawing. The school-room, school-house, play-ground, the home, maps of the city or village and district furnish the material for mechanical and free-hand drawing. Pupils who have a special talent for drawing should be allowed to push their work further than the rest of the class.

Industrial drawing and space teaching (*Raumlehre*) demand special attention.

f. REALIEN. The *realien* include geography, history, and natural history.

GEOGRAPHY. The children should be made acquainted with the home, the Fatherland the German Empire and the principal countries of the earth. They learn the position of the continents and of the principal heavenly bodies. Instruction in geography is principally synthetic. It must be studied through representations of the teacher upon the blackboard, through maps, charts and globes.

Middle Class (two hours). Instruction begins in this class with a description of the school-house, the home and the district. Next comes the government district, and then the province. The pupils learn also the boundaries of the Fatherland, the provinces with principal cities, the chief rivers and mountains.

Advanced Class (two hours). Review of what has been learned in the middle class. Special attention is now paid to Prussia, the German Empire and Austria. Other

---

* The outline here given preceded the general introduction of Stuhlmann's system, reference to which will be found in the second chapter.

European countries are next studied. Pupils learn name, position, boundaries, the most important rivers, mountains and cities.

The geographical position, boundaries, chief cities, mountains and rivers of other important countries of the world are taken up, more especially those countries which, through their history, culture or commerce, occupy prominent positions.

In mathematical geography, the following instruction is recommended:
1. Touching the horizon;
2. Touching representations of the earth, and the significance of the most important lines and points.
3. Touching the form and shape of the earth;
4. Touching the motions of the earth;
5. Touching the seasons and zones;
6. Touching the fixed stars;
7. Touching the sun and moon;
8. Touching the calendar.

HISTORY. This instruction includes the history of Prussia and the German Empire. The aim of this instruction is to develop patriotism and loyalty toward the royal family. Instruction in history is given by the teacher in the form of talks. History and geography should go hand in hand.

Middle Class (two hours). The children learn the names of the emperor and empress, the crown-prince and the most important men of the day. The teacher relates anecdotes of these men and remarkable periods of their lives.

The pupils are next made acquainted with the chief events in the reigns of Frederick William IV and Frederick William III. The great men of these reigns are held up to the pupils with their peculiar traits.

Thereupon the children study some of the most important events in former reigns and in the history of the chief *Kurfürsten*.

Advanced Class (two hours). Instruction is given in the early history of Germany and Brandenburg. Here only the most remarkable events are touched upon. From the time of the Thirty Years' War, however, instruction is systematic and connected.

In addition to the above, some of the most important inventions and discoveries both in ancient and modern times are taken up.

NATURAL HISTORY. The aim of this instruction is to acquaint the children with those phenomena in nature which are daily before their eyes. It is one of the most important duties of the teacher to awaken an interest in nature, to train the powers of observation, that the pupils see how much cause for reflection is given by her products and the workings of her forces.

This instruction in natural history should follow the object method. Practical experiments, when possible, are to be most highly commended.

The middle and advanced classes receive together two hours a week of instruction in natural history.

Middle Class (one hour). In summer, the children learn some of the important plants of the garden, the fields and the woods. In teaching, the teacher should have before him the plant itself or a good representation of the same.

In the winter, the children study some of the *Mammalia* and *Aves*, usually the domestic animals.

A few minerals of the district are taken up.

Advanced Class (one hour). Physiology and hygiene. The structure of the human body and the fundamental laws of health. Knowledge of plants, animals and minerals is extended.

In the vegetable kingdom, the most important are fruit trees, grains and the ordinary vegetables used for food. Useful trees, shrubs, herbs and poisonous plants are studied. Growth and conditions of growth of plants require attention, as do also the cultivation and fertilization of the field.

Foreign and domestic products, such as cotton, tea, coffee and sugar, should be studied.

The proper division of the vegetable kingdom for the elementary schools is into (1) trees, (2) shrubs, (3) herbs, (4) grasses, (5) mushrooms, (6) mosses.

The animals studied by the children are brought under the following classification: (1) mammalia, (2) aves, (3) amphibia, (4) fishes, (5) insects, (6) worms, (7) mollusks, (8) infusoria. Foreign words are seldom used in classification.

The animals worthy of special consideration are those useful or dangerous to man; those which by size, construction or peculiarities awaken a high degree of interest. Examples—the butterfly, bee, ant, tape-worm, trichina.

Middle Class (one hour). In nature the pupils take up the most important peculiarities of air, heat, water, vapor, fog, clouds, dew, frost, rain, snow, hail, ice and storms.

The practical application of natural forces is considered, as in the gun, pumps, etc.

Advanced Class (one hour). In this division are studied the barometer, fountains and water-conduct; the ear, echo, musical instruments; the thermometer, steam engine, manufacture of gas; the effects of light and shade; colors, the mirror, the burning-glass, eye-glass, the eye and sight, the rainbow; the pully, the lever, the scales, gravitation.

Electricity and magnetism are taught in connection with the most common applications of these forces. Pupils are given a general idea of the electric telegraph. All this work is to be treated by the object method in a simple manner.

9. MUSIC. Vocal music is an important factor in education. It ennobles character by cultivating a taste for that which is beautiful. The pupil takes with him into life a number of songs, which will not only be a source of pleasure to him through life, but will also tend to lessen the influence of corrupt popular songs upon the general public. With this end in view, the greatest care should be taken in the selection of the songs to be learned in school. The preference should be given to those songs which awaken a love of the Fatherland.

Lowest Class (one hour). Exercises to train the voice and ear. The children learn to sing after the teacher distinct tones in the middle register to the different vowels. The pentachord, both rising and falling, is practiced to various texts. The text of songs is read aloud by the teacher and explained. The pupils then learn the same by heart. A few simple songs should be well studied in this division.

Middle and Advanced Classes (two hours). Continuation of the above. Diphthongs are practiced in different pitches. Then follow vowels and diphthongs in connection with consonants, next syllables and words. The pentachord is extended to the scale. The chord of three and four notes is presented in different keys.

From twenty to thirty songs are practiced in addition to the religious music. Songs are sung in unison and by ear. Singing by note and in two parts can only be practiced under especially favorable conditions. A secular or religious song should begin or close all school sessions. In this way songs are best fixed in the memory of the pupils.

h. GYMNASTICS *(two hours).*
Middle and Advanced Classes.
1. Exercises upon the horizontal bar, and in standing.
2. Exercises with a stick; high jumping.
3. Exercises in drilling, and upon the parallel bars.
4. Exercises in hopping, and upon the horizontal bar.
5. Exercises in walking, and in broad jumping.
6. Exercises in running, and upon the parallel bars.

Simple gymnastic exercises for the lowest class should be given in the pauses.

i. MANUAL TRAINING FOR THE GIRLS *(two hours).* *Middle and Advanced Classes.* The end of this instruction is to fit the girls for domestic life. Industry should be encouraged, and a taste for neatness in personal appearance and economy in clothing. The following should be taught:

a. Knitting. Pupils should learn to do all work of this kind required in ordinary domestic life.

b. Sewing. Pupils should learn the different plain stitches and patching.

c. Easy work in sewing and stitching articles of clothing, etc., outlining, darning.

d More difficult work in sewing and stitching articles of clothing, the cutting of linen.

Fancy stitches should not be taught in the elementary schools. Practical plain sewing is the aim of the course. With this end in view the children should repair and make articles of clothing under the direction of the teachers, bringing the necessary materials from home.

It is not enough for the teacher to show how a thing is to be done. The pupils' work must be carefully controlled, and they must be taught the technical terms necessary to express intelligently what they are doing.

Local school authorities decide as to the necessity of instruction upon the sewing-machine.

The teacher should keep a record of the work done by pupils[*]

---

[*] There are many manuals of industrial work for girls. That of Agnes Schallenfeld, published in Frankfurt-on-the-Main, is in quite general use.

Time-tables for Ungraded Schools (*Einklassige Volksschulen*).

A.

HOURS.	Monday.	Tuesday.	Wednesday.	Thursday.	Friday.	Saturday.
MORNING.						
8– 9	Religion, I, II, III	Language, I, II, III	Religion, I, II, III	Language, I, II, III	Religion, I, II, III	Religion, I, II, III
9–10	Language, I, II, III	Arithmetic, I, II, III	Language, I, II, III	Arithmetic, I, II, III	Language, I, II, III	Language, I, II, III
10–11	Geography, I, II	History, I, II	Natural History, I, II	Geography, I, II	History, I, II	Natural History, I, II
11–12		Religion, I, II	Gymnastics, I, II		Music, II	Gymnastics, I, II
AFTERNOON.						
2–3	Drawing, I	Geometry, I		Drawing, I, II	Language, I, II, III	
	Language, II, III	Language, II, III		Language, III		
3–4	Arithmetic, I, II, III	Music, I, II, III		Language, I, II, III	Arithmetic, I, II, III	

B.

HOURS.	Monday.	Tuesday.	Wednesday.	Thursday.	Friday.	Saturday.
MORNING.						
8– 9	Geography, I, II	History, I, II	Natural History, I, II	Geography, I, II	History, I, II	Natural History, I, II
9–10	Religion, I, II, III	Religion, I, II, III	Geometry, I	Religion, I, II, III	Religion, I, II, III	Religion, I, II
10–11	Language, I, II, III	Language, I, II, III	Language, I, II, III	Language, I, II, III	Language, I, II, III	Language, I, II, III
11–12		Drawing, I, II, III	Gymnastics, I, II		Music, I, II	Gymnastics, I, II
AFTERNOON.						
2–3	Language, I, II, III	Music, I, II, III		Language, I, II, III	Drawing, I	
					Language, II, III	
3–4	Arithmetic, I, II, III	Arithmetic, I, II, III		Arithmetic, I, II, III	Arithmetic, I, II, III	

I. Advanced class.   II. Middle class.   III. Lowest class.

II. THE HALBTAGSSCHULE (THE HALF-DAY SCHOOL).

As previously stated, these schools are permitted only under exceptional circumstances, that is, when the number of pupils exceeds eighty or the school accommodations are not sufficient for eighty pupils in one room, and conditions are not favorable for the appointment of a second teacher.

The two classes in these half-day schools receive together thirty-two hours a week of instruction. This time is divided as follows:

	Lower Class.	Higher Class.
Religious instruction	2	3
Language, realien*	7	10
Arithmetic, geometry	3	4
Music	0	2
Drawing	0	0
Gymnastics	0	1
	12	20

In addition to the above, two hours a week are devoted to the manual training for girls.

The course of study for ungraded schools is followed as closely as the limited time will permit.

III. COURSE OF STUDY FOR SCHOOLS WITH TWO DEPARTMENTS.

1. For the Primary Department:
    a. Lower Class, twenty-two hours per week.
    b. Higher Class, twenty-eight hours per week.
2. For the Advanced Department:
    a. Lower Class, twenty-eight hours per week.
    b. Higher Class, thirty-two hours per week.

This time is to be divided as follows:

	PRIMARY DEPARTMENT.		ADVANCED DEPARTMENT.	
	Lower Class.	Higher Class.	Lower Class.	Higher Class.
a. Religious instruction	4	4	4	4
b. Language	11	8	8	8
c. Arithmetic	4	4	4	4
d. Geometry	0	0	0	2
e. Drawing	0	2	2	2
f. Realien (history, geography, natural history)	0	6	6	8
g. Music	1	2	2	2
h. Gymnastics, manual training	2	2	2	2
	22	28	28	32

* The *realien* embrace geography, history and natural history.

Instruction is to be given according to time-tables. The local school inspector (*Lokalschulinspektor*) can authorize changes in time-tables which do not alter the total number of hours; other changes must be authorized by the government.

Pupils are divided into classes, according to progress, as follows:

PRIMARY DEPARTMENT. The lower class has two divisions; at first, in arithmetic and reading, three divisions. These are the children of the first and second years. The higher class in the primary department is composed of the children of the third year.

ADVANCED DEPARTMENT. The lower class is composed of the children of the fourth and fifth years. The higher class is made up of the sixth, seventh and eighth years, with two subdivisions in grammar and arithmetic.

For use in teaching, the following are necessary.

1. In the primary department:
   a. A copy of each text and reference book used in the department;
   b. Large wooden or paste-board alphabets for teaching reading;
   c. A numerical frame;
   d. A wall map of the home province;
   e. Charts for use in teaching natural history;
   f. Rule and compass;
   g. Two large blackboards.
2. In the advanced department:
   a. A copy of each text and reference book used in the school;
   b. A globe;
   c. A wall map of Germany;
   d. A wall map of Europe;
   e. A wall map of Palestine;
   f. A wall map of the home province;
   g. Plates for use in teaching natural history;
   h. A violin;
   i. Rule and compass;
   j. Bodies for use in teaching geometry;
   k. Two large blackboards.

In Protestant schools, a bible and a copy of the song book used in the district.

There must be a thermometer in each class-room, a likeness of the Emperor, and in Romish schools, a crucifix.

TEACHERS' RECORDS - - The teacher must keep a school register, showing daily attendance and weekly progress of pupils. The principal must keep also a history of the school district.

The time-tables and course of study for the year must always be in each school-room.

The following are the necessary books and stationery:
(1) The primer and readers;
(2) Arithmetics;
(3) Song book;
(4) Books for religious instruction;
(5) Slate, pencil, sponge, rule and compass;
(6) Blank books for use as
   a. Diary;
   b. Copy book (for penmanship);
   c. Copy book (for orthography and language exercises);
   d. Drawing book (for the upper classes).

Lessons should be carefully prepared by each teacher.
Younger teachers should use pen or pencil in this preparation. All work of pupils should be conscientiously regulated and supervised.

Syllabus of work.

a. RELIGIOUS INSTRUCTION (not given).
b. LANGUAGE. Correct oral and written expression of thoughts which enter into the life of the people, and ability to read good literature with profit are the aims of language work. Special attention should be paid to ordinary business forms.
PRIMARY DEPARTMENT.
Lower Class (eleven hours). Object method. The pupils are led to talk of objects within their line of vision. The powers of observation are trained by study of objects in their vicinity. School, play-ground, garden, field, forest and home afford a great variety in the material for this instruction.
Enunciation and expression receive attention.
In teaching reading and writing, the method of the normal school of the district is to be followed The alphabet method is strictly forbidden.
At the close of the first six months, the pupils must be able to divide simple statements into words, the words into syllables, the syllables into their respective sounds. They must be able to make and read the letters representing these sounds.
At the close of the first six months the pupils learn the printed characters and the names of the letters of the alphabet.
From the outset, to prevent mechanical reading, children should be taught to associate words, and, later, statements with the objects or ideas they represent.
Each selection read must be thoroughly understood by the pupils.
Simple proverbs, aphorisms and short easy selections should be learned by heart, and repeatedly reviewed.
In teaching writing, the teacher should show upon the blackboard the formation of the letters.
Orthography is encouraged through careful attention to enunciation, attentive reading, copying and dictation.
From the very beginning, children, in writing, should be taught to use the proper punctuation.
At the close of the second school year, the children should be able to read with facility and correctness the selections they have taken; to answer simple questions as to subject-matter; to reproduce these selections orally; to copy correctly from the primer and to write from memory the proverbs and sayings learned by heart. They should have had simple exercises in dictation.
Higher Class (eight hours). In this class the reader for middle classes is used.
The instruction of the lower class is continued, with closer attention to subject-matter and expression.
Pupils are led to reproduce orally selections read. At first they will confine themselves quite closely to the words of the book. The teacher, by judicious questioning, will force pupils to express themselves more or less in their own words.
Selections in prose and poetry are to be learned by heart.
Orthography is continued as in the lower class.
Special attention is now given to
1. The use of capital letters;
2. The shortening and lengthening of vowels;
3. The *Umlautung*;
4. Hard and soft consonants at the beginning of words and syllables;
5. The finding of final consonants through lengthening words;
6. The use of the letters t, th, dt; f, v, ph, pf; s, chs, cks, gs, ts, z.
In writing, the forms of the German script alphabet are now taught in regular order. The pupils learn the comparative size and position of letters, the proper distance between letters and between words. Time writing is then practiced in concert.
The formation of the plural of nouns is taught. Statements are formed with personal pronouns and verbs in the present tense, and, afterward, in the past and future tenses.
Adjectives are studied in the same way.
Word-building, effect of affixing the syllables *chen, lein, er,* and *in* to nouns; *ig, lich* and *isch* to adjectives; of prefixing the syllable *un* to adjectives.
ADVANCED DEPARTMENT.
Lower Class (eight hours). The pupils read the more difficult selections of the middle-class reader. Correct expression and a thorough understanding of the subject-matter are required. Pupils have now acquired the ability to reproduce selections from reader orally with facility, and to repeat readily that which has been learned by heart.
For practice in orthography, the selections learned by heart are written from memory and corrected by book. Simple rules are learned.
Writing is continued as above.
Pupils learn to compare adjectives and to form the indicative and imperative modes of verbs. They are drilled in the declension of nouns with and without definite and indefinite articles. All the work should be practical, the pupils forming statements and simple sentences introducing the various forms of words desired. Sentences are transposed, and the subjunctive mode is introduced.
Word building is continued. Words not understood by the pupils are best defined by practical examples, *i. e.,* the teacher forms sentences introducing such words.
The pupils learn the parts of a simple sentence.
The pupils reproduce in writing short stories told by teacher, selections from the reader, etc.
Closer attention is given to form and style of oral expression. Composition receives attention. An effort is made to teach pupils to express themselves in writing correctly

and clearly. At first the teacher places outlines upon the blackboard. Little by little these outlines disappear, and the pupils are led to depend more and more upon themselves, after teacher has explained orally the work required of them.

Higher Class (eight hours). The reader for advanced classes is now studied. At least thirty selections are mastered yearly. The first step toward the proper understanding of a selection lies in reading same aloud faultlessly and in speaking upon its subject-matter. The greatest care must be given to correct expression.

Oral reproduction exercises are continued with greater strictness, the teacher ever requiring more and more of the pupils.

A number of poems, especially songs of the people, are learned by heart.

Before leaving school, the pupils should be able to read understandingly the more difficult selections, which, in subject matter, are not too far above them. They should be able to express clearly and correctly the subject-matter of such selections.

Reading and the other language exercises should enable the pupils to spell and punctuate correctly. Should the same faults often occur, the teacher must devote special attention thereto. Words alike in sound and foreign words in common use demand special drill.

In penmanship the German and Latin scripts are practiced at stated hours. Proverbs and sayings of the people serve as copies.

Pupils must learn to write neatly and legibly.

The different forms of sentences are studied with reference to punctuation; parts of speech, the formation and use of participles; the declension of adjectives with and without definite and indefinite articles; the declension of pronouns; prepositions and their uses; government of verbs and adjectives; conjugation of verbs; analysis of sentences; direct and indirect discourse; word-building.

All the work is introduced and practiced with practical examples.

In composition the reproduction exercises are continued and short themes are written on familiar subjects. Pupils are often asked, at the close of a lesson in natural history, geography, the history of the Fatherland and religion, to write what they have learned.

Careful attention is paid to ordinary business forms, letters, bills, notes, receipts, etc. Letters are prepared ready to post.

All written work should be done neatly.

c. ARITHMETIC. The pupils should acquire a thorough knowledge of practical business arithmetic. They must be trained to give reasons for steps in the solution of problems. Mechanical work must be excluded. Pupils should be most carefully drilled in the German coinage, weights and measures. Long rows of figures beyond the comprehension of the pupils should be avoided, and attention paid to that which will be of use to pupils in trade or in every-day life.

In introducing new processes mental should precede written work in all classes.

PRIMARY DEPARTMENT.

Lower Class, Second Division (four hours). Object teaching. The numbers from one to ten. Use of a variety of objects, marks, lines, crosses, etc. The numerical frame. The four fundamental processes from one to ten.

Lower Class, First Division (four hours). Numbers one to 100. A variety of simple problems, embracing these numbers.

Higher Class (four hours). The numbers up to 1000. The four processes are exercised by problems in mental arithmetic up to 1000, especially, however, up to 200. Coinage, weights and measures.

ADVANCED DEPARTMENT.

Lower Class (four hours). A careful review of the work of the three preceding years. Practice in written work beyond the number 1000. The mental and written solution of a variety of simple problems in the four processes.

Higher Class, Second Division (four hours). Common and decimal fractions. The drill in common fractions should be confined quite closely to those fractions which occur in common business transactions (one-half to one-twelfth). Special care should be taken in teaching the reduction of common to decimal fractions, and this solution of problems, involving unusual common fractions, is recommended.

First Division (four hours). Computation of time, ratio and proportion, percentage, interest, discount, profit and loss, alligation, area of surfaces and contents of solids.

d. GEOMETRY.

ADVANCED DEPARTMENT.

Higher Class (two hours). This instruction should be connected with drawing on the one hand and arithmetic on the other. By the former pupils learn to represent correctly lines, surfaces and solids; by the latter they understand how to compute the length of lines, the area of surfaces and the contents of solids.

This instruction should be practical to meet the needs of tradesmen and farmers.

The course includes lines, angles, triangles, quadrilaterals, polygons, circles and the regular solids.

e. DRAWING.* Training of the eye and hand is the object of this course. A taste for symmetry, regularity and beauty of form should be cultivated. Instruction should be practical, the aim being to afford assistance to those especially who will learn a trade.

PRIMARY DEPARTMENT.

Higher Class (two hours). Drawing begins in this class and consists of mechanical work, with slate, rule and pencil, in copying lines and figures drawn upon the blackboard by the teacher. Lines of different length and position, triangles and quadrangles are drawn, then simple objects, as table, chair, desk, etc.

ADVANCED DEPARTMENT.

Lower Class (two hours). The above work is continued, partly with paper and pencil. Pupils now commence free-hand drawing, continuing mechanical drawing. Lines and angles are drawn and then divided into a given number of equal parts. Parallelograms and simple geometrical figures are drawn.

---

*The outline here given preceded the general introduction of Stubhmann's system, reference to which will be found in the second chapter.

Higher Class (two hours). Free-hand drawing is continued, and pupils with a special talent for this work are permitted to go further than the others. Industrial drawing, however, is the most important. The school-room, school-house, play-ground, the home, maps of the city or village and district furnish the material for both mechanical and free-hand drawing.

The close relation between the instruction in drawing and geometry (*Raumlehre*) should never be lost sight of.

f. REALIEN. The *Realien* include geography, history and natural history.

GEOGRAPHY. The children should be made acquainted with the home, the Fatherland, the German Empire and the principal countries of the earth. They study the continents and the principal heavenly bodies. The instruction is largely synthetic and must be given through representations of the teacher upon the blackboard, through maps, charts and globes.

PRIMARY DEPARTMENT.

Higher Class (two hours). Instruction begins in this class with a description of the school-house, the home and the district. Next comes the government district, and then the province. Pupils study elementary geographical charts.

ADVANCED DEPARTMENT.

Lower Class (two hours). Continuation of above, with more detailed description of the government district and province. Pupils learn the boundaries of the Fatherland, the provinces, with their principal cities, the chief rivers and mountains.

Higher Class (two hours). Special attention is now paid to Prussia, the German Empire and Austria. Other European countries are next studied. Pupils learn name, geographical position, boundaries, the most important rivers, mountains and cities.

The geographical position, boundaries, chief cities, mountains and rivers of other important countries of the world are taken up, more especially those which, through their history, culture or commerce, demand especial attention.

In mathematical geography the following instruction is recommended:
1. Touching the horizon;
2. Touching representations of the earth, and the significance of the most important lines and points;
3. Touching the form and shape of the earth;
4. Touching the motions of the earth;
5. Touching the seasons and the zones;
6. Touching the fixed stars;
7. Touching the sun and moon;
8. Touching the calendar.

HISTORY. This instruction includes the history of Prussia and the German Empire. The aim of this instruction is to develop patriotism and loyalty toward the royal family.

Instruction in history is given by the teacher in the form of talks. History and geography should go hand in hand.

PRIMARY DEPARTMENT.

Higher Class (two hours). The children learn the names of the emperor and empress, the crown-prince, and the most important men of the day. The teacher relates anecdotes of these men and important events in their lives.

The pupils are next made acquainted with the chief events in the reigns of Frederick William IV and Frederick William III. The great men of these reigns are held up to the pupils, with their peculiar traits.

ADVANCED DEPARTMENT.

Both Divisions together (two hours). The pupils study a few of the important events in the early history of Germany and Brandenburg. From the time of the Thirty Years' War instruction is systematic and connected.

In addition to the above, some of the most important inventions and discoveries, both in ancient and modern times, are taken up.

NATURAL HISTORY. The aim of this instruction is to acquaint the children with those phenomena in nature which are daily before their eyes. It is one of the most important duties of the teacher to awaken an interest in nature, to train the powers of observation, that the pupils see how much cause for reflection is given by her products and the workings of her forces.

This instruction in natural history should follow the object method. Practical experiments, when possible, are strongly recommended.

PRIMARY DEPARTMENT.

Higher Class (two hours). The pupils learn some of the important plants of the garden, the fields and the woods. The teacher should have before him the plant itself or a good representation thereof. In the winter the children study some of the mammalia and aves, usually the domestic animals.

ADVANCED DEPARTMENT.

Lower Class (two hours). Knowledge of plants, mammalia and aves is extended. In summer a few insects are studied; also amphibia and fishes. Attention is now given to the manner of living of the animals studied. The growth of plants and their uses are talked of. Peculiarities in the forms of plants and the bodies of animals are described.

A few minerals of the district receive attention.

Higher Class (two hours). Physiology and hygiene. The structure of the human body and the fundamental laws of health. Knowledge of plants, animals and minerals is extended. Useful trees, shrubs, herbs and poisonous plants are studied. Growth and conditions of growth. The cultivation and fertilization of the field.

Foreign and domestic products, such as cotton, tea, coffee and sugar should be studied.

The proper division of the vegetable kingdom for the elementary schools is into (1) trees, (2) shrubs, (3) herbs, (4) grasses, (5) mushrooms, (6) mosses.

The animals are brought under the following classifications:
(1) mammalia, (2) aves, (3) amphibia, (4) fishes, (5) insects, (6) worms, (7) mollusks, (8) infusoria. Foreign words are seldom used in classifications.

Mammalia and aves demand special attention, much less amphibia and fishes. The insects are also important. Animals useful or dangerous to man; those which, by size or peculiarities, awaken a high degree of interest should be studied.

Home minerals alone are studied.

ADVANCED DEPARTMENT.

Higher Class (two hours). In nature the pupils take up the important peculiarities of air, heat, water, vapor, fog, clouds, dew, frost, rain, snow, hail, ice and storms.

The practical application of natural forces is considered, as in the gun, pumps, etc.

Next require attention the barometer, fountains and water conduits; the ear, echo and musical instruments; the thermometer, steam engine, manufacture of gas; the effects of light and shade; colors, the mirror, the burning glass, eye glasses, the eye and sight, the rain-bow; the pulley, the lever, the scales, gravitation.

The ordinary applications of electricity and magnetism are taken up. Pupils are given a general idea of the electric telegraph.

All this work is to be treated by the object method in a simple manner.

g. MUSIC. Vocal music is an important factor in education. It ennobles character by cultivating a taste for the good and beautiful. The elementary school graduate takes with him into life a number of songs, which will not only be a constant source of pleasure to him, but will also tend to lessen the influence of corrupt popular music. With this end in view the greatest care should be taken in the selection of songs. The preference should be given to those which foster a love of the Fatherland.

PRIMARY DEPARTMENT.

Lower Class (one hour). Exercises to train the voice and ear. The children learn to sing after the teacher distinct tones in the middle register to the different vowels. The pentachord, both rising and falling, is practiced to various texts. A few simple songs, if possible, within the compass of the pentachord, are practiced. The text of songs is read aloud by the teacher and explained. The pupils then learn the same by heart. A few simple songs should be learned in this division.

Higher Class (two hours). Continuation of the above. Diphthongs are practiced in different pitches. Then follow vowels and diphthongs in connection with consonants, then syllables and words.

ADVANCED DEPARTMENT.

Lower Class (two hours). Continuation with special reference to purity, flexibility and correct tone color. The pentachord is extended to the scale. The chord of three and four notes is presented in different keys. The pupils learn about twenty-five secular and religious songs.

Higher Class (two hours). Continuation of above. The more difficult intervals, the minor chord of three and four notes and a few songs in minor keys are practiced. Scales and chords of three and four notes in different keys receive attention. Pupils are more carefully drilled in the singing of songs. They learn about thirty secular and religious songs. Singing is in unison, though part singing is not excluded. If instruction has been given systematically from the first, it will be possible for the pupils to obtain some knowledge of notation and also learn to sing by note.

h. GYMNASTICS.

PRIMARY DEPARTMENT *(two hours).* Simple gymnastic exercises in preparation for the

ADVANCED DEPARTMENT *(two hours).* The boys have
(1) Exercises in standing and upon the horizontal bar;
(2) Exercises with a stick, high jumping;
(3) Exercises in drilling, and upon the parallel bars;
(4) Exercises in hopping, and upon the horizontal bar;
(5) Exercises in walking, and in broad jumping;
(6) Exercises in running, and upon the parallel bars.

i. MANUAL TRAINING FOR THE GIRLS (two hours). The end of this instruction is to fit the girls for domestic life. Industry should be encouraged, and a taste for neatness in personal appearance and economy in clothing. The following should be taught.

a. Knitt ng. Pupils should be able to do all work of this kind required in ordinary domestic life;

b. Sewing. Pupils should learn the different plain stitches and patching;

c. Easy work in sewing and stitching articles of clothing, etc., outlining, darning;

d. More difficult work in sewing and stitching articles of clothing, etc., the cutting of linen.

Fancy stitches should not be taught in the elementary schools. Practical plain sewing is the aim of the course. With this end in view, the children should repair and make articles of clothing under the direction of the teacher, bringing the necessary material from home.

It is not enough for the teacher to show how a thing is to be done. The work of pupils must be carefully controlled, and they must be taught the technical terms necessary to express intelligently what they are doing.

Local school authorities decide as to the advisability of instruction upon the sewing machine.

The teacher should keep a record of the work done by the pupils.

IV. THE SCHOOL WITH THREE CLASSES AND TWO TEACHERS.*

When, in a school with two classes and two teachers, the number of pupils exceeds 120, a third class is to be formed.

---

* The course of study for schools with two classes and two teachers is followed as closely as circumstances permit.

The third class has twelve hours' instruction weekly; the second class twenty-four, and the first class twenty-eight. This time is divided as follows:

	Third Class.	Second Class.	First Class.
Religious instruction	2	4	4
Language	7	8	8
Arithmetic	2	4	5
Geometry			
Drawing	0	1	1
Realien (geography, history and natural history)	0	4	6
Music	1	1	2
Gymnastics, manual training	0	2	2
	12	24	28

Instruction should follow the time-table. Changes not affecting the number of hours may be authorized by the local school inspector (*Lokalschulinspektor*). Other alterations must be authorized by the government.

The children are divided into classes according to progress in studies.

The third class embraces the children of the first school year; the second class, those of the second, third, and fourth school years; the first class, children of the four following years.

There should be two divisions of the first and second classes.

Teachers must have the following articles:

(1) In the third class.
   a. A copy of the primer used in the school;
   b. Alphabetical charts for use in teaching reading;
   c. A numerical frame;
   d. A rule;
   e. A large portable blackboard.

(2) In the second class:
   a. A copy of each book used in the class;
   b. A wall map of Palestine;
   c. A wall map of the home province;
   d. Natural history charts;
   e. Rule and compass;
   f. Two large portable blackboards.

(3) In the first class:
   a. A copy of each book used in the class;
   b. A globe;
   c. A wall map of Germany;
   d. A wall map of Europe;
   e. A wall map of Palestine;
   f. Natural history charts;
   g. A violin;
   h. A rule and compass;
   i. Bodies for use in teaching geometry;
   j. Two large portable blackboards.

In Protestant schools.
   k. A Bible;
   l. A copy of the song-book used in the district.
 Each class-room must be furnished with a thermometer, a likeness of the Emperor, and Roman Catholic schools with a crucifix.
 TEACHERS' RECORDS. Each teacher must keep a register, showing daily attendance and weekly progress of pupils. The principal is to keep a history of the school district. The course of study and time-table for each class must be kept constantly in each class-room.
 BOOKS, ETC. The pupils of this school require
 (1) The primer and readers;
 (2) The primary arithmetic;
 (3) Song-books;
 (4) Books for religious instruction;
 (5) Slate, pencil, sponge, rule and a pair of compasses;
 (6) Blank books:
   a. Diary;
   b. Copy book;
   c. Composition book;
   d. Drawing book.

V. THE SCHOOL WITH THREE CLASSES AND THREE TEACHERS.

The third class has twenty-two hours' instruction weekly; the second class has twenty-eight hours' instruction weekly; the first class has thirty-two hours' instruction weekly.

The time is divided as follows:

	Third Class.	Second Class.	First Class.
	Hours.	Hours.	Hours.
Religious instruction	4	4	4
Language	11	8	8
Arithmetic	4	4	4
Geometry	0	0	2
Drawing	0	2	2
Realien (geography, history and natural history)	0	6	8
Music	1	2	2
Gymnastics, manual training	2	2	2
	22	28	32

The third class embraces children of the first and second years.
The second class embraces children of the third, fourth and fifth years.
The first class embraces children of the sixth, seventh and eighth years.
The regulations touching books, etc., for pupils and teachers, teachers' records, etc., are the same as those for schools with three classes and two teachers.

VI. THE SCHOOL WITH FOUR DEPARTMENTS.

The fourth class has twenty-two hours of instruction per week; the third class has twenty-eight hours of instruction per week; the second

class has twenty-eight hours of instruction per week; the first class has thirty-two hours of instruction per week.
This time is divided as follows:

	Fourth Class.	Third Class.	Second Class.	First Class.
	Hours.	Hours.	Hours.	Hours.
Religious instruction	4	4	4	4
Language	11	8	8	8
Arithmetic	4	4	1	1
Geometry	0	0	0	2
Drawing	0	2	2	2
Realien (geography, history, natural history)	0	6	6	8
Music	1	2	2	2
Gymnastics, manual training	2	2	2	2
	22	28	28	32

Each class has a two years' course, and is composed of two divisions. The regulations governing teachers' records, etc., books, etc., for teachers and pupils are the same as in other schools.

VII. THE SCHOOL WITH FIVE DEPARTMENTS.

The fifth class has twenty-two hours of instruction per week;
The fourth class has twenty-two hours of instruction per week;
The third class has twenty-eight hours of instruction per week;
The second class has twenty-eight hours of instruction per week;
The first class has thirty-two hours of instruction per week.
This time is divided as follows:

	Fifth Class.	Fourth Class.	Third Class.	Second Class.	First Class.
	Hours.	Hours.	Hours.	Hours.	Hours.
Religious instruction	4	4	4	4	4
Language	11	11	8	8	8
Arithmetic	4	4	1	1	1
Geometry	0	0	0	0	2
Drawing	0	0	2	2	2
Realien (geography, history, natural history)	0	0	6	6	8
Music	1	1	2	2	2
Gymnastics (manual training)	2	2	2	2	2
	22	22	28	28	32

The fifth and fourth classes have each a course of one year.
The third, second and first classes have each a course of two years.
The three upper classes have each two divisions.
Regulations are the same as for other schools, touching school furniture, teachers' records, books and supplies for teachers and pupils.

VIII. The School with Six Classes.

The sixth class has twenty-two hours of instruction per week;
The fifth class has twenty-two hours of instruction per week;
The fourth class has twenty-eight hours of instruction per week;
The third class has twenty-eight hours of instruction per week;
The second class has thirty hours of instruction per week;
The first class has thirty-two hours of instruction per week.
This time is divided as follows:

1. In the sixth and fifth classes: Hours.
   Religious instruction 4
   Language 11
   Arithmetic. 4
   Music 1
   Gymnastics (manual training)... 2
                                                    22

2. In the fourth and third classes:
   Religious instruction.. 4
   Language 8
   Arithmetic 4
   Drawing. 2
   Realien (geography, history and natural history) 6
   Music.............. 2
   Gymnastics (manual training)......................... 2
                                                     28

3. In the second class:
   Religious instruction............... 4
   Language 8
   Arithmetic. 4
   Drawing... 2
   Realien (geography, history and natural history)........ 8
   Music 2
   Gymnastics (manual training) 2
                                                     30

4. In the first class:
   Religious instruction........................... 4
   Language.. 8
   Arithmetic.. 4
   Geometry... 2
   Drawing. 2
   Realien (geography, history and natural history)........ 8
   Music 2
   Gymnastics (manual training)........................ 2
                                                     32

The children of the sixth, fifth, fourth and third classes are those of the first, second, third and fourth school years. The course is one year in each class. The children of the second and first classes are those of the fifth and sixth, the seventh and eighth school years. The course is two years in each class.

There are two divisions in each of the two upper classes.
Regulations touching school furniture, supplies, teachers' records, etc., are the same as those in other schools.

IX. TABLE SHOWING THE RELATIVE DISTRIBUTION OF PRUSSIAN ELEMENTARY PUBLIC SCHOOLS IN 1886.*

	Number of pupils.	Per cent.
I. Ungraded schools	1,146,602	23.70
II. Half-day schools (*Halbtagsschulen*)	571,474	11.81
III. Schools with two classes and two teachers	415,116	8.58
IV. Schools with three classes and two teachers	186,772	10.06
V. Schools with three classes and three teachers	277,015	5.73
VI. Schools with four or more classes	1,941,268	40.12
	4,838,247	100.00

Sixty-four thousand seven hundred and fifty regular teachers were employed; 57,902 were males, 6,848 were females.† In New York public schools in 1886, 31,325 teachers were employed; 5,952 were males, 25,373 were females.

DIVISION OF THE SCHOOL CHILDREN ACCORDING TO SEX.

Boys	2,422,044
Girls	2,416,203
Total	4,838,247

IN MIXED CLASSES.

Boys	1,766,807
Girls	1,745,343
Total	3,512,150
In Classes of Boys	655,237
In Classes of Girls	670,860
Total	4,838,247

DIVISION OF CHILDREN ACCORDING TO RELIGION.

Protestant (*evangelisch*)	3,062,856
Roman Catholic (*katholisch*)	1,730,402
Other Christian denominations (*sonst christlich*)	9,569
Jewish (*jüdisch*)	35,420
Total	4,838,247

Eleven and eighty-one hundredths per cent of all children in attendance upon the public elementary schools received instruction in *Halbtagsschulen* (Half-day schools). These schools were classed among the normal divisions of Prussian elementary schools by decree of October 15, 1872. This step was taken under the firm conviction

---
* From "Preussische Statistik 101." Berlin, 1889.
† There were also 1,183 assistant teachers in addition to those of industrial training for girls.

that a teacher with a limited number of pupils of one grade can accomplish more in a few hours than with an overcrowded class of all grades in double the time. "*Es wird angenommen, dass ein Lehrer in wenigen Stunden mit einer kleineren Zahl einer Altersstufe angehöriger Kinder mehr erreiche, als mit der doppelten Zahl der Stunden in überfüllter Klasse mit Kindern aller Altersstufen.*" This expedient merits attention in New York, in districts not provided with sufficient school accommodations.

Between May 20, 1886 and October, 1888, 354 new public elementary schools were opened with 975 classes, 788 male and 164 female teachers and 57,017 pupils.*

SEVENTH CHAPTER.
SCHOOLS PREPARATORY TO THE NORMAL, FOR MALES.
Präparandenanstalten.

Most of these preparatory schools are the outgrowth of private undertakings. Teachers began by taking a few pupils to fit for the normal schools. From 1872 to November, 1888, thirty-two of these institutions were founded by the government. At this date there were 1,991 pupils in attendance. There are also similar private schools which receive State aid.

There are, as a rule, two teachers at each of these institutions. The principal receives from $450 to $600 a year, and lives in the school; the assistant from $300 to $450, and ten per cent of salary as allowance for rent.

The male teachers are now quite generally prepared for the normal schools in these Präparandenaustalten, though some enter directly from the Mittelschulen, Realschulen, Gymnasien or after preparation in private.

Before admission to Präparandenaustalten candidates must have mastered the elementary school *curriculum* of eight years.

Except under unusual circumstances candidates are admitted only once a year, at Easter time or Michaelmas.

All applicants must present:

a. Certificate of baptism.
b. Certificate of vaccination and good physical condition.
c. Certificate as to educational qualifications and moral character.
d. Statement of father that he will pay costs of tuition, etc., with certificate from proper authorities that he possesses sufficient means to do so.

Candidates are then admitted to the entrance examination, which is both written and oral, and embraces the course of study for elementary schools.

The number of pupils is generally between fifty and seventy, divided into two classes. The course covers three years. The second class has one division and should be absolved in one year. Promotion to the first class follows upon examination. The first class consists of two divisions generally instructed together.

---

*Since 1871 the experience of elementary school teachers has averaged about 17.5 years. The following is the table for 1871:

Per cent.
Experience of from one to ten years 39.21
Experience of from eleven to twenty years 23.28
Experience of more than twenty years 37.51

The pupils are prepared for the normal school. The tuition is nine dollars a year.

These institutions are day schools, the pupils themselves providing for board, clothing, books, etc.

Candidates without means pay no tuition and receive aid to meet other expenses.

Examinations are held at the close of each term.

Semi-annual reports of studies and deportment are given to the pupils. These must be returned with signature of father or guardian.

Admission to the normal school follows upon examination. Candidates who fail must return to the preparatory school. The course of study is arranged to permit the entrance to the normal school at Easter or Michaelmas.

Course of Study.

REMARKS. Object.—The preparation of candidates for the professional training of the normal school. Instruction is given in religion, language, mathematics, history and geography, natural history, penmanship, drawing, vocal music, instrumental music (piano, violin, organ) and in French. All subjects are obligatory except French and instruction upon the piano and organ.

Instruction is to be given in a simple manner, objectively when possible. Pupils should be trained to observe closely and to think for themselves. Careful attention should be paid to correct enunciation and expression.

The pupils are encouraged to make collections of minerals, insects, etc.

RELIGION (not given).

LANGUAGE. The private reading of pupils is carefully overlooked.

Correct, easy and logical oral and written expression is the aim of the course in language. Pupils should be able to read well and reproduce, in their own words, difficult selections in poetry and prose, when the subject-matter is not too technical.

Reading. This is based upon the readers. The selections chosen should include the most important styles of prose and the principal forms of poetry. Something should be read from each celebrated national author.

Selections are studied as follows:
 a. Reading aloud by the teacher;
 b. Explanation of figures of speech and difficult expressions;
 c. Repeated reading by the pupils with especial reference to correct enunciation and expression;
 d. Subject-matter and train of thought;
 e. Free reproduction of the subject-matter, either in abbreviated form or with addition of that read between the lines; also with different dispositions of the subject-matter as to form and style;
 f. Oral and written explanation of figures of speech, difficult or technical expressions, synonyms, comparisons and the like.

Explanation of the form of selection and short sketches of the author are given. A number of poems are learned by heart.

The readers embrace also historical and geographical selections and natural history. These are carefully considered as well.

Second Class (two hours per week). Short stories, fables, parables, sayings, historical anecdotes, descriptions, geographical pictures, lyrical poems and songs and biographical sketches.

First Class (weekly two hours). In addition to the above proverbs and aphorisms, songs and elegies, legends and ballads, idyls and selections from dramas.

Biographical sketches of the lives of celebrated authors, such as Luther, S. Dach, Paul Gerhard, Gellert, Lessing, Claudius, Klopstock, Voss, Herder, Schiller, Goethe, Postalozzi, M. Arndt, Schenkendorf, Koerner, Rückert, Uhland, Chamisso, Freiligrath, Geibel, Grimm, Hebel, Krummacher.

Remark. The course in the first class is two years. Selections are to be made so that in the second year the same forms of prose and poetry occur, but not the same pieces.

LANGUAGE (continued). Style is formed by written tasks taken from the reader, from the instruction in geography, history, or natural history, or from life. The subject-matter for this written work is first taken up orally in the class.

Second Class (two hours a week). Every three weeks two exercises are corrected by the teacher.

First Class (one hour per week). Every two weeks an exercise is corrected by the teacher. These exercises consist of historical sketches, short biographies, geographical descriptions, character description, explanation of synonymous expressions, proverbs, sayings and letters.

Remark. In addition to these written exercises the second class must absolve a complete course in orthography involving the rules of orthography and practice to fix these rules in mind.

The first class repeats these rules with their application.

GRAMMAR. The children learn the laws for the use of the mother tongue.

Second Class (one hour per week). Simple, compound and complex sentences; parts of speech.

First Class (one hour per week). Composition of words and sentences; punctuation.

Private reading. The school library contains geographical and historical matter, biographies of celebrated men, popular sketches, German classics and translations of foreign classics, all of which come within the range of the pupils. The selection of the books to read is made by the pupils with the advice of the teacher. Generally, a book is read every fortnight. For practice in oral expression, the pupils must repeat before the class short episodes, descriptions, etc., of that which they have read.

MATHEMATICS. The pupils must acquire readiness in the solution of problems in arithmetic and algebra. Pupils must always be able to give reasons for each step in the solution of a problem. Repeated drill is given to fix processes in the minds of pupils.

Second Class (weekly three hours). Formation of figures. Notation and numeration. The four fundamental processes, decimals, and common fractions. Simple algebraic problems.

First Class (weekly two hours). Simple problems in algebra continued. Proportion, interest, discount, partnership, alligation, extraction of square root.

GEOMETRY. Surfaces and solids. Simple propositions and definitions of lines, angles, triangles, quadrangles, polygons and the circle. Computation of areas and contents.

Second Class (one hour per week). Instruction should be given objectively. Care should be paid to correct expression. Practice in constructing geometrical figures. Properties of lines, angles, triangles and quadrangles. Construction and computation. Divisions of solids. Properties of prisms, pyramids, cylinders, spheres and the regular solids. Computation of contents.

First Class (two hours per week). Planimetry. Lines, angles, parallel lines, figures in general and triangles in particular.

First Division. The most important propositions touching parallelograms and the circle. Practice in construction and computation.

HISTORY. The most important facts in ancient, especially Grecian and Roman History. The birth and spread of Christianity. The migration of tribes. The principal persons and facts in German History, and that of Brandenburg and Prussia.

The subject-matter is introduced by the teacher in the form of talks, the pupils learning to connect same with important persons and facts. Reproduction exercises by the pupils. The principal dates, figures and names are learned by heart and fixed through repeated drill. Historical selections from readers add interest to this instruction.

Second Class (two hours per week). The peoples of the Orient, the Greeks and Romans; birth and spread of Christianity; the ancient Germans; the migration of tribes; the empire of the Franks; Mahomet.

First Class (two hours). Pictures of mediæval and modern times.

GEOGRAPHY. The pupils learn particularly the geography of the home province, Germany and Europe; generally that of the other parts of the globe, including the five oceans and the elements of mathematical geography.

Instruction proceeds from the known to the unknown. Globes, charts and pictures should be largely used. Pupils must learn to draw maps of what has been studied. Useless details involving names and figures should be avoided.

Second Class (two hours). Form, shape and motions of the earth considered generally. Construction of maps, showing principal lines. Divisions of water and land. The geography of the home province.

First Class (two hours). Geography of Germany and Europe in particular, and that of Asia, Africa, America and Australia in general. Continuation of mathematical geography.

NATURAL HISTORY. The construction, peculiarities, manner of living, etc., of the principal animals. The elements of Physics and Chemistry through experimentation. Plants.

Second Class (two hours per week). Vegetable physiology and zoölogy. The most important plants of the neighborhood. Representatives of each class in the animal kingdom.

PHYSICS AND CHEMISTRY *(one hour per week).* Weight, warmth, cohesion, adhesion, compression of air, magnetism and electricity. Introduction to chemistry. Chemical terminology.

First Class (three hours per week). Pupils of the first and second years:
Review of the plants and animals considered above. Classification of the same.
Pupils of the first year:
Physiology. Structure of the human body.
Pupils of the second year:
The most important minerals.
Pupils of the first year:
Weight, magnetism and electricity, oxygen, hydrogen, nitrogen, carbonic acid gas, sulphur, phosphorus and chlorine, with their principal combinations.
Pupils of the second year:
Sound, light, warmth, metals and their combinations.

WRITING. Pupils must write neatly, legibly and with facility. They must learn to write well upon the blackboard.

The formation of letters. Practice in copy-books and upon the blackboard. Corrections should be made principally in the class. Faults of pupils should be clearly explained. Attention is first paid to neatness, legibility and correctness, then to rapidity.

Second Class (two hours weekly). The German script.
First Class (one hour weekly). The Latin and German scripts.

DRAWING. Mechanical and free-hand drawing. Training of the eye and hand. Development of taste for regularity, symmetry and beauty of form. Facility in drawing geometrical figures and simple objects in nature.

The whole class should work together, that which is to be drawn being first explained by teacher. Children should be led by questions to discover their own faults and correct the same. Practice upon the blackboard.

Second Class (two hours per week). Straight lines varying in length, position and thickness. Division of these lines into parts. Angles and division of the same into parts. Symmetrical figures drawn within squares. Curved lines, and figures with curved lines.

First Class (two hours per week). Drawing of right-angled bodies and circular bodies before the eyes of pupils. Drawing of symmetrical figures, characteristic forms of plants and simple work in ornamental drawing.

MUSIC. *I. Vocal.* Pupils should learn by heart about twenty religious and secular songs. They should learn to read at sight easy hymns and songs of the people. Texts of songs are carefully explained. Attention is then devoted to key, rhythm, interval and time. The proper breathing places are indicated.

At the beginning of each lesson a scale is practiced or an exercise in finding different intervals is studied.

The two classes are combined and have two hours instruction weekly. The songs and hymns to be practiced are definitely stated.

II. Instrumental, piano. The pupils learn to play well all major and minor scales, also easy studies, sonatinas and sonatas. In each piece careful attention is given to key, rhythm and time. A new piece is first played with one, then with two hands. Good position of hand and arm, precision of touch and ease of execution are attended to.

Pupils are divided according to capacity. Each division has one hour per week. Attention is given to careful graduation of the work.

III. Violin. The principal major and minor scales in the first position. Facility in playing hymns and songs previously practiced. Ability to read easy music at sight. Most careful attention to holding of instrument; to good and easy bowing; to firm position of the first finger; to style and correctness in playing in concert.

Pupils are divided according to capacity. Each division has one hour per week.

IV. Music in general. Pupils learn the different clefs, rhythms and keys, the usual foreign terms and definitions of time, the doctrine of intervals and tone relations. One hour of instruction weekly.

By examples upon the blackboard the proper understanding is facilitated and the pupil thereby led to the independent solution of given tasks. The basis of instruction in this branch is Widmann's "Harmony, Melody and Form," and, chiefly, Draht's "Theory of Music."

V. Harmony. The pupils learn to name and play in all positions and inversions the major and minor triad, and the chord of the dominant seventh. The formation of the triads and seventh chord is explained upon the blackboard and instrument, and fixed by repeated drill in the different keys. One hour of instruction weekly for each class.

VI. Organ. Pupils learn the elementary manual and pedal exercises; to play at sight four-part hymn tunes and to play from memory easy selections.

Careful attention should be given to fingering, change of fingers on the same key, playing together with two hands, use of pedals (heel and toe). Necessary instruction in the use of stops is given.

The first exercises should be most carefully drilled.

The pupils are divided according to capacity. Each division has one hour of instruction weekly. The school for the organ of Schütze and the preludes of Baumert.

FRENCH. Pupils are permitted to take this course only when all other work is thoroughly satisfactory.

The pupils study carefully a French Elementary Grammar, learning to translate easy exercises from German into French and from French into German.

Drill in punctuation and orthography. Rules are always fixed in mind by practical examples. From the beginning pupils are taught to understand easy sentences in French, and later questions. The simplest rules give material for comparison of the two languages. The selections in reader are first translated literally, then into good German, finally re-translated into French. These selections afford subject-matter for dialogues with the pupils, bringing into practice the words and rules learned.

Second Class (weekly, two hours). Lessons 1-59. Elementary Grammar by Ploetz. Drill upon all forms of *avoir* and *être.* After finishing the first forty lessons, the first and second conjugations are learned.

First Class (weekly, two hours). Lessons 60-91. Ploetz, Elementary Grammar. Thorough drill of the four conjugations. Division A finishes the elementary reader.

GYMNASTICS. Candidates learn all exercises included in the "*Neuer Leitfaden für den Turnunterricht in den Preussischen Volksschulen*" (New Manual for Gymnastic Instruction in Prussian Elementary Schools). Each hour of instruction in gymnastics begins with exercises standing, then moving and drilling, finally with gymnastic apparatus.

All pupils work together two hours a week in gymnastics, following the manual.

EIGHTH CHAPTER.

NORMAL SCHOOLS FOR MALE TEACHERS.*

Normal schools are called teachers' seminaries in Prussia. They are smaller and more numerous than our own.

In October, 1888, there were 107 State normal schools for males in Prussia, with an attendance of 8,507, of which number 3,031 were day

---

*Formerly many male elementary teachers were not graduates of normal schools. The fact that all are now held rigidly to the same requirements has driven almost all to the normal schools. "Es giebt für alle Lehrer nur einen Weg der Vorbildung. Dieselbe wird ihnen im engsten Anschlusse an die Aufgaben, bezw. an den Lehrplan der Volksschule ertheilt, indem sie sich auf Vertiefung und Ergänzung der dort gewonnenen Kenntnisse beschränkt." (Drs. Schneider and Petersilie.)

students. Except in seven cases, no normal school had more than 100 pupils; thirty-five had less than seventy; thirty-eight were for boarders only; thirty-two had day pupils alone, and thirty-seven had both.

With several exceptions, all normal schools are situated in small villages. As a rule, they are not as well built or furnished as similar institutions here. There are always one or more practice-schools connected with each institution.

There are 165 practice-schools (*Uebungsschulen*) in connection with the normal schools; 19,760 pupils were in attendance in 1886. These schools had 478 classes, 159 for boys, 36 for girls, and 283 mixed classes.

Upon entering the normal schools, pupils must have had a good common school education, and, excepting pedagogics, must be familiar with the subject-matter of all branches taught. This accounts in a large measure for the thoroughness of the professional training received.

Tuition is free at all normal schools. In boarding-schools, lodging, heating and light are free. Candidates without means receive further aid — in boarding-schools, amounting to twenty-two dollars and fifty cents; in day-schools, to thirty-seven dollars and fifty cents annually. Graduates are bound to serve at least three years subject to the direction of the government, under the penalty of forfei'ing the cost of instruction and living expenses advanced. Tuition in such cases is reckoned at fifteen dollars annually.

Students are generally sons of farmers, tradesmen or teachers. Few come from higher ranks of society.

Each normal school has a director, a first teacher, four ordinary teachers and an assistant.

In addition to free dwelling or the legal allowance therefor, the salaries paid are as follows:

Director	$900 to	$1,200
First teacher	675 to	825
Ordinary teachers	425 to	675
Assistant	300	

Teachers are generally either clergymen or former high and elementary school instructors.

Opportunity is afforded the members of the faculty to visit other normal schools. Through conferences and school revisions normal school teachers are brought frequently in contact with elementary teachers.

Examinations for admission to the normal schools are held once each year before the beginning of the term. Candidates of good moral character and good physical condition not under 17 years of age, nor more than 24, possessing means to meet expenses, are admitted to this examination, whether prepared in middle schools, Realschulen, Gymnasien, Präparandenanstalten or in private.

Applications must be made at least three weeks before the examination. More than three trials are not permitted.

With the application, candidates must present:
1. Certificate of baptism (birth certificate);
2. Certificate of vaccination and good physical condition;

3. Certificate as to moral character;

4. Statement, legalized by local authorities, of father or guardian that means are at hand to pay living expenses.

Special permission of the provincial school consistory (*Provinzial-Schulcollegium*) is required for the admission of candidates more than 24 years of age.

Candidates who pass the entrance examination before appointment are reëxamined as to physical condition by the normal school physician. The examination is conducted by the normal school faculty with a commissary of the provincial school consistory as chairman. School commissioners and preparatory school teachers (*Präparandenbildner*) of the district may be present.

The examination is both oral and written. In the written examination the candidate must write a short theme upon a given subject, and answer a number of questions covering the subject-matter of the examination. These questions should not require more than two or three minutes' time each. The committee is authorized to shut out from further examination pupils who show themselves deficient in the written work. The oral examination covers all subjects taught in the normal school, except pedagogics. Each normal school teacher examines in the subject in which he instructs in the normal school. The whole faculty of the normal school should be present. When this is not the case, the candidates should be classed according to the number of teachers present; nevertheless, when difference of opinion exists as to maturity of candidate for normal school, he must be reëxamined in doubtful subjects before the whole faculty.

The principal subjects are: 1. Religion; 2. Language; 3. Arithmetic and Geometry; 4. Music; 5. Realien and History. (Realien, *i. e.*, Geography and Natural History.)

Candidates who fail in any one of these subjects will be received only when all other work attains a high degree of excellence. When an imperfect examination in music is attributable to lack of ear, the candidate may be received. Failure in the examination upon the organ is not sufficient cause for debarring a candidate.

This entrance examination must prove proficiency of pupils, as follows:

a. RELIGION. (Not given);

b. LANGUAGE. 1. Parts of speech, composition of words and analysis of sentences. The candidate must be able to give practical applications of rules in proverbs, or quotations from national authors;

2. He must be able to read readily at sight, with correct enunciation and expression. He must explain what he has read, defining words and analyzing sentences;

3. He must know the principal forms of poetry, and recognize the same. He must be able to repeat from memory poems of Schiller, Uhland, Rückert, etc., with good expression, explaining the subject-matter;

4. He must be able to write correctly and grammatically, and compose short themes on given subjects.

c. ARITHMETIC. Facility and correctness in the solution of problems in mental arithmetic; a thorough knowledge of the method of solution upon the blackboard.

The four fundamental processes, common and decimal fractions, ratio and proportion, business arithmetic, including alligation. Problems in elementary algebra.

The candidate must work with facility and surety, showing that he understands reasons for processes used.

d. GEOMETRY. Elements of plane geometry. Computation of area of surfaces and contents of solids.

e. GEOGRAPHY. General knowledge of the parts of the globe and the five oceans, more particular knowledge of Europe, especially Germany. The principal points in mathematical geography.

f. HISTORY. Principal events in ancient history, such as the Trojan war, the Persian wars, the bloom of Greece, Alexander the Great, the foundation of Rome, the Kings, expulsion of the Tarquins, Camillus, the Gauls, the Punic wars, etc. The birth and spread of Christianity, the migration of tribes; principal persons and events in the history of Germany, Brandenburg and Prussia up to date. The most important dates only are desired.

g. NATURAL HISTORY. The candidate must prove his knowledge of the three kingdoms by the explanation of important specimens of each class under adopted classifications. More detailed information is required touching the cultivated and poisonous plants, the *fauna* and *flora* of the home. The elements of chemistry. It is desirable that candidate prepare for examination by practical course in experimentation.

h. PENMANSHIP. Ease in correct writing on paper and on the blackboard. All written work must be orderly, neat and legible.

i. DRAWING. Free-hand and mechanical drawing. Practice required in blackboard drawing.

j. MUSIC. Candidates must be able to sing, from memory, with a fair degree of correctness, twenty of the best known secular and religious songs. They must be able to read at sight simple hymns and songs of the people.

Candidates should be able to play correctly on the piano all major and minor scales; to play from memory easy studies and sonatas; to read, at sight, simple selections. They should play readily and correctly upon the violin the most important major and minor scales in the first position. Hymns and songs, learned by heart, must be played from memory, and easy music at sight. A good foundation in the *technique* of the instrument is the first requisite.

In general musical knowledge, the examination covers clefs, rhythms and keys, the usual foreign terms and definitions of time, the doctrine of intervals and tone relations.

In harmony, candidates must name and play the major and minor triad and the chord of the dominant seventh in all positions.

In organ-playing, the candidates must know the elementary manual and pedal exercises, play simple four-part hymns at sight and simple selections from memory.

k. GYMNASTICS. Candidates must be ready to perform all exercises contained in the "New Manual for Gymnastical Instruction in Prussian Elementary Schools."

ORGANIZATION OF NORMAL SCHOOLS AND COURSES OF STUDY.

Each normal school should be connected with a graded and ungraded practice school.

The work in the practice school is under the charge of the director of the normal school, through a special teacher as *Ordinarius.*

The position of *Ordinarius* is given to one of the normal school instructors.

The course in the normal school covers three years.

In the third class, the pupils do not teach in the practice school. An effort is made toward uniformity, to prepare the class, as a unit, for professional training. Introduction to pedagogics.

In the middle class the pupils extend their knowledge of all subjects which they are to teach. They are present at classes in the practice school, attending carefully to the instruction given, assisting the teacher and conducting themselves class exercises. Continuation of pedagogics.

In the highest class, the pupils finish the course of study at the normal school, receiving instruction for subsequent work in preparation for the final examination, which occurs not less than two nor more than five years after graduation. They are given systematic instruction in the practice school under the oversight of the *Ordinarius*. No pupil should have less than six or more than ten hours per week as teacher. Before graduation each one must have instructed at least in arithmetic, religion, language, music, and one of the other subjects. There must be, at least three times a year, a change in the division of work. Before such change the pupil must conduct an examination in the presence of the normal school faculty.

The teacher must keep a register, showing in detail the work which has been accomplished by weeks. This serves as the basis for reviews and examinations. Examinations are held at the close of each term. They embrace all subjects taught, and are held in the presence of the normal school faculty. If pupil is not ready for promotion he should leave the school. Permission may be given, however, to repeat the work of his class, if good reasons make same advisable.

The following shows the weekly distribution of time in the various subjects:

	First year.	Second year.	Third year.
Pedagogics	2	2	3
Religion	4	4	2
Language	5	5	2
History	2	2	2
Arithmetic and algebra	3	3	1
Geometry	2	2	1
Natural history, chemistry and physics	4	4	2
Geography	2	2	1
Drawing	2	2	1
Writing	2	1	0
Gymnastics	2	2	2
Instrumental and vocal music	5	5	3
Foreign tongues (English, French, Latin)	3	3	2
	38	37	22

Wednesday and Saturday are half-holidays. An opportunity is thus afforded for excursions to collect plants, minerals, etc. The vacations amount to eight weeks annually.

All subjects embraced in elementary school work and pedagogics are compulsory for all pupils.

According to decree of 1878, dispensations in music should be limited as much as possible.

Instruction in French, English and Latin is voluntary. Pupils who have never studied one of these languages previous to entrance to the normal school are permitted to begin only in exceptional cases. The preference is generally given to French.

The instruction received at the normal school should conform to that which the pupils will afterward give as teachers. The subject-matter should be carefully arranged by the teacher and as carefully reproduced by the pupil.

Dictation is forbidden, also copying during the lectures. Text-books should serve as the basis of instruction, so far as possible, in each subject.

Method always accompanies subject-matter. Pupils are carefully drilled in oral and written reproduction of lessons.

In addition to a good working library the normal school should have a physical and, when possible, a chemical laboratory. The school should be provided with the necessary objects used in teaching.

The ibrary should be well classified. It should contain the German classics, both in prose and poetry, with which the pupils are to become acquainted; pedagogical works, particularly those of the last 300 years — for example, the Pedagogical Library of Karl Richter; the best books for the young from the time of the philanthropists to the present; finally, the popular books upon universal and national history and natural history, descriptive works, etc.; Schleiden, Tschudi, Masius, Brehm, Rossmässler, Russ, Hartwig, Müller, Von Barnhagen, Adami, Werner Hahn, Ferd. Schmidt, Wildenhahn, W. Baur, Freitag, Riehl, etc.

Private reading of pupils is systematic and controlled. It is ordered so that they must read necessary works, such as Lessing's Minna von Barnhelm, Schiller's Wallenstein, Goethe's Hermann und Dorothea, Pestalozzi's Lienhard und Gertrud.

Associations of pupils for self-improvement, such as common reading, musical exercises, botanical excursions, etc., are encouraged.

At least once a month the pupils have a holiday to devote to such independent work as they see fit. Upon these days teachers should not assign special tasks.

The time-tables should be so arranged that the practice school may not interfere with other work. The first class receives instruction when the practice school is not in session; the second class partly so.

Instruction in the normal school is given in accordance with a special course of study for each school. The following syllabus serves as the guide for such courses of study:

SYLLABUS OF WORK.

PEDAGOGICS.

Third Class (two hours weekly):
The pupils learn the most important features in the history of education through pictures of famous educators, notable periods, the most interesting and useful improvements in elementary schools. This instruction is completed by the introduction of the

chief pedagogical works, especially those published since the Reformation. Reading centralizes around some important pedagogical question until same be understood by pupils in all its bearings.

Second Class (two hours weekly):
General principles of education. Instruction. Form in which instruction should be given. Development through instruction. Reference is made to logic and psychology.

First Class (three hours weekly):
Methods. The teacher's position. School government. School organization. School law. The third hour is devoted, in the practice school, to practical applications of methods learned by the pupils.

RELIGION.
(Not given.)

LANGUAGE.

Third Class (five hours weekly):
a. Grammar: Simple, complex and compound sentences. Parts of speech, declensions, comparison of adjectives, conjugations. The rules of orthography and punctuation.
b. Reading: Practice in reading aloud and in written expression, form and construction of poetry, meter, rhyme; lyric and epic poetry; the poetical narrative, legend, saying, fairy tale, ballad; didactical forms, fable, parable.

Second Class (five hours weekly):
a. Grammar: More difficult work in the analysis of sentences. Composition of words. Rules relating to verbs, adjectives and prepositions. Punctuation.
b. Reading, as above, with more difficult selections. Lyric, epic and dramatic poetry in general. Songs of the people, odes, ballads, romances, epics and dramas.
c. Method in teaching reading: Practical application in the form of class exercises.

First Class (two hours):
Review. Extension of the matter in reading. Method in language work in connected form, illustrated by class exercises.
In language work careful attention should be paid to:
a. Fluent and correct expression of thought.
b. Correctness in written expression of thought, clearness in form and good arrangement. The pupil must learn to teach that which he has been taught. To insure this, ease and correctness in oral and written expression are necessary.
c. Private reading. The books read should embrace the master-pieces of national authors both in prose and poetry.
d. Reading in class. Pieces are selected from the time of Luther to the present. Form and subject-matter are taken up. Selections in readers in use in elementary schools are carefully studied. A number of poems are learned by heart.
In addition to the readers in use in the practice school, there are special normal school readers.

HISTORY.

Third Class (two hours weekly):
Pictures in ancient history, especially the history of Greece (a, age of the heroes; b. period of the law-givers; c. the Persian wars to the death of Alexander the Great). Rome (a, the Kings; b. the Republic; c. the fall of the Republic and the first century of the Empire).

Second Class (two hours weekly):
Country of the ancient Germans; wars with the Romans; the migration of tribes; period of the Carlovingians, especially the spread of Christianity and Charlemagne; history of the early German dynasties; the Crusades to the time of the Reformation.

First Class (two hours weekly):
The history of Brandenburg and Prussia up to date; relations with neighboring States and countries.
Method begins in the third class with drill in relating historical facts and events; continues in the second class with class exercises; closes in the first class with systematic work in the practice school.

ARITHMETIC AND ALGEBRA.

Third Class (three hours weekly):
The formation of figures; the four fundamental processes; decimals; common fractions, ratio and proportion; business arithmetic, including alligation, square and cube root.

Second Class (three hours weekly):
Proportions; positive and negative terms; equations of the first degree, powers and roots.
Class exercises are given, the subjects being taken from elementary school courses of study. Pupils learn use of numerical frame and other apparatus for teaching primary arithmetic.

First Class (one hour):
Review to fix method. Equations of the second degree and, if possible, progressions and logarithms. Drill to insure ease and security in the solution of problems.

GEOMETRY.

Third Class (two hours weekly):
The triangle, the parallelogram and the circle. Exercises in construction.

Second Class (two hours weekly):
Instruction as to the equality and similarity of plane figures and their computation. Computation of contents of solids.

First Class:
Review with special reference to method in teaching.
In all classes pupils are drilled in the drawing of geometrical figures upon the blackboard.
The instruction is based upon text-books, and is given objectively. Clear instruction is given upon methods of teaching, suggestions as to continuation of course and ability to impart instruction.

NATURAL HISTORY, PHYSICS AND CHEMISTRY.

Third Class (four hours weekly):
 a. Natural History: The study of selected indigenous plants belonging to the commonest families. The system of Linné. Botanical morphology.
 In the winter, zoölogy two hours weekly.
 b. Physics: Magnetism, electricity and mechanics.
 c. Chemistry: The principal bases and their combinations, especially in relation to mineralogy. Two hours per week.

Second Class (four hours weekly):
 a. Natural History: Study of the principal forms of seed and spore plants. System of classification. Form, growth and diffusion of plants.
 In the winter, knowledge of zoölogy is extended. Structure of the human body and conditions of health. Two hours a week.
 b. Physics: Light, heat and sound.
 c. Chemistry: Extension of above. Organic chemistry. Two hours a week.
 Methods of teaching these subjects receive careful attention through lectures and class exercises.

First Class (two hours weekly):
 Review and completion of the course, with special attention to methods of teaching. Geology is introduced and suggestions given to aid in continuing the study.
 Instruction is to be given objectively. Physics and chemistry should not be taught without practical experimentation; botany and zoölogy without objects or good representatives of objects studied. Pure mechanical work in memorizing is forbidden.

GEOGRAPHY.

Third Class (two hours weekly):
 The geography of the home province, Prussia, Germany and the rest of the globe, the former particularly, the latter superficially. The study of maps.

Second Class (two hours weekly):
 Germany and Europe. Mathematical geography. Method in teaching geography through lectures and class exercises.

First Class (one hour weekly):
 Continuation of methods. The use of atlas, wall-maps, globes, tellurians and other objects employed in teaching geography. Each pupil must have a good hand atlas for use in this work. The school text-book is an abbreviated edition of the complete work.

DRAWING.

Third Class (two hours a week):
 Free-hand drawing. Lines and angles. Division of the same into parts. Drawing of geometrical figures and symmetrical figures within squares. Drawing of sections of right-angled bodies and circular bodies before the eyes of pupils. Drawing of symmetrical and ornamental figures. Mechanical drawing with rule and compass. Practice in ornamental drawing. Practice in drawing upon the blackboard.

Second Class (two hours a week):
 a. Elements of perspective; b. free-hand drawing with black chalk, bister, sepia, etc., from plaster of Paris models and from nature. This work should be arranged according to the respective talents of pupils; c. practice in drawing upon the blackboard.

First Class (one hour weekly):
 a. Continuation of work as above, especially as regards blackboard drawing, giving attention to work in drawing demanded in teaching other subjects; b. Method in teaching drawing; c. Suggestions to aid in continuing the work beyond the normal school course.
 Instruction in drawing should enable pupils to do all work neatly required in teaching this and other subjects, such as geometry, geography, etc.

PENMANSHIP.

Third Class (two hours weekly); Second Class (one hour weekly):
 The object of this course is to insure:
 1. Neatness, facility and correctness in all written work;
 2. A definite method for use in teaching penmanship.

GYMNASTICS.

The basis of the course in gymnastics is the "New Manual for Instruction in Gymnastics." Pupils may be brought further than the book goes. They must be able to teach systematically all exercises included in said manual.
 The third and second classes have two hours of practical gymnastics per week, the first class one hour. The first class has, in addition, instruction of one hour weekly upon the structure of the human body, expedients in the case of accidents, the history and purpose of physical training, apparatus used in gymnastic exercises.
 Pupils of the first class, under oversight of the teacher of gymnastics, give instruction in the practice school.

MUSIC.

I. PIANO. Technical exercises, in the third class, in touch and execution. A systematic course of instruction as given in the best schools for the piano. Independent pieces beginning with Clementi's Sonatinas, or something similar, and progressing in such a way as to introduce, in addition to the classics, modern works.

Second Class. Continuation of above. Talented pupils study the works of Cramer. Sonatas by the classical masters, such as Mozart, Beethoven, Hayden, etc., systematically arranged by teacher.

First Class. Practice upon the piano in private.

II. ORGAN. Pupils are advanced according to capacity and previous preparation in the school for the organ followed.

Third Class. Continuous practice in the hymn-book used.

Second Class. Practice of the simple organ movements which have been analyzed and transposed in the course in harmony. Playing such selections at sight. Entire acquisition of a prelude to each one of the customary hymn-tunes, as preparation for appropriate playing of organ during divine service.

First Class. Transposition of melodies, modulation. Composition of short preludes and simple interludes.

III. HARMONY. Pupils who are not to qualify themselves as organists must nevertheless absolve the work of the third class and the historical part of that of the first class.

Third Class. Construction and practice of major and minor triads; of the chords of the seventh and ninth as to chief forms and fundamental laws of their construction.

Second Class. Drill in the knowledge of the harmonized material and continuous employment thereof in the harmonization of tunes and in the analysis, transposition and practice of short harmonized organ movements given by teacher. First course in modulation.

First Class. Harmonization of hymn-tunes and songs of the people. Composition of simple preludes to hymn-tunes and formation of appropriate interludes. Second course in modulation. Ancient modes. General study of the most important forms of vocal and instrumental music. Construction and care of the organ. Outlines of the history of music.

IV. VIOLIN. Pupils are classified according to capacity. Each division must absolve the course. The following directions require attention:
  a. Drill in committing to memory the hymns and songs of the people studied;
  b. Drill in duets;
  c. Introduction in the advanced divisions to the higher positions.

V. SINGING. Special instruction for the third class in the formation of the voice. Hymn-tunes and songs of the people, at first in one, then in two and three parts.

Mixed chorus with classes combined.

Progressive instruction of the elementary classes in:
  a. *Vocalises* and *solfeggi* properly so called and composed in the form of complete pieces;
  b. More and more detailed knowledge of intervals, but chiefly of the chords and their various forms.

Entire acquisition of the hymns and psalms most in vogue. Hymn-tunes and other songs in several parts.
  a. The liturgical chorus which the first class learns to lead;
  b. Other religious choral songs, *motettes*, psalms by classical masters;
  c. Secular choral songs, especially the best of folk and national songs;

Special instruction for the first class in method of teaching music in elementary schools, connected with exercises in the practice-school. Execution of mixed choral songs in combination with the upper class of the practice school.

The object of the course is the training of teachers for good work in teaching music in the elementary schools, not to develop special talents at the expense of the other pupils. Pupils are taught to love the old masters and beware of introducing their own compositions in their school districts.

FOREIGN TONGUES.

There are three courses of three, three and two hours per week respectively, divided not according to years but according to progress of pupils. In the lowest class the course begins with an introductory grammar of the language studied, French, English, or Latin.

GARDENING, FRUIT TREES, SILK CULTURE.

In the instruction given in natural history, these subjects require special attention.

NINTH CHAPTER.

EXAMINATIONS FOR MALE TEACHERS.

I. FIRST TEACHERS' EXAMINATION FOR TEMPORARY LICENSES IN ELEMENTARY SCHOOLS.

At the close of the normal school course, an examination is held to test the qualifications of candidates for a temporary engagement as teacher.

Applicants not graduates of normal schools, but who are at the end of the twentieth year of age, are admitted, upon presentation of certificates, testifying to good moral character and physical condition.

All candidates must give notice at least three weeks before the time set for the examination, forwarding the following certificates:
1. Certificate of baptism (birth certificate).
2. Certificate of good physical condition.
3. Certificate of good moral character.

In every case, an autobiography is to be inclosed with the above certificates. Said certificates must be official.

The committee in charge of the examination is composed of the commissary of the provincial school consistory as chairman, a member of the local government, the director and teachers of the normal school for the district in which the examination is held. The school commissioners may be present, and also other persons when authorized by the chairman.

Candidates not trained in normal schools must submit drawings and written specimens of their work. The other candidates must submit the drawing and writing-books of the last year at the normal school.

The written test consists of:
1. A theme on methods, school organization or management, or from the province of instruction in language or literature.
2. An essay on some subject connected with religious instruction.
3. The complete solution of three problems in arithmetic and geometry.
4, 5, 6. Answer to one question in each of the three subjects — natural history, history and geography.
7. For those who are to give instruction upon the organ, the harmonization of a choral with prelude and interludes.

The voluntary subjects are:
8. English, French or Latin. Translation of a selection from one of these foreign tongues into German, and translation of German into the foreign tongue in question.

Four hours are allowed for the first task and two hours for each of the others.

The subjects are chosen by the member of the provincial school consistory, upon recommendation of the normal school faculty.

The practical test consists of a class exercise in one of the compulsory subjects. This work is assigned two days in advance, and candidate must submit a written analysis thereof.

Those examined in voluntary subjects must give a class exercise in said subjects when possible.

The oral examination embraces all subjects taught in the normal school, covering the entire normal school course. The chairman is authorized, however, to exclude such work as he deems unnecessary. The candidate must answer questions definitely and clearly.

When written work is exceptionally good, candidates may be excused from a part or the whole of the oral examination.

In the case of Jewish candidates, the subject of religion is not touched upon.

The oral examination must be held in the presence of the whole committee.

A record is kept of the standing of applicants in each subject; marks, very good, good, sufficient, not sufficient, as the case may be. Candidates fail to pass who do not attain the mark "sufficient" in religion, German, arithmetic and more than three of the other subjects (pedagogics, singing, drawing, writing, history, geography, natural history, geometry).

Candidates who pass the examination receive a certificate stating preparation candidate has had for the examination and standing attained in each subject.

The committee then licenses said candidates to teach provisionally.

II. THE SECOND AND FINAL TEACHERS' EXAMINATION FOR ELEMENTARY SCHOOLS.

Not earlier than two years nor more than five years after the first examination, teachers must pass the final examination. They are then assured of pay for life, even should the schools where they are employed cease to exist.

The committee is the same as that for the first examination.

Candidates must give notice to provincial school consistory, through the school commissioner, at least four weeks before the examination. They must submit:

1. A certificate from the school commissioner;
2. An essay, stating authorities used, and certifying that they have received no assistance from other sources;
3. A drawing, with certificate that candidate has received no assistance in preparing the same;*
4. A specimen of penmanship under the same conditions.

These four particulars determine the admission or non-admission of candidates to the examination.

Candidate may endeavor to raise the standing attained at the first teachers' examination, or he may try the voluntary subjects.

The written test consists of a theme on some subject connected with school management, a theme relating to religious instruction, and one touching instruction in one of the other common school branches. Jewish candidates substitute another subject in place of religious instruction. This work is chosen by the chairman of the examining committee upon recommendation of the normal school faculty for the district in which the examination is held. The work must be done in the presence of a member of the committee.

The practical test consists of a class-exercise, the subject for which is announced the day before.

The oral test covers the history of education, principles of education, school management and methods of teaching. At the discretion of the committee, questions may be asked touching positive knowledge of subject-matter.

Candidates are marked, very good, good, sufficient, not sufficient, as the case may be.

Candidates who fail to attain the mark "sufficient" in the class-exercise are rejected. Results in other respects are determined as at the first examination.

Successful candidates receive certificates showing standing attained in each subject. The committee then licenses said candidates to teach permanently.

* This drawing is now submitted by the candidate in person at the time of the examination.

Candidates failing to attain a higher standing than at the first examination in the subjects in which they have been reëxamined are, nevertheless, permanently licensed, if other work has been satisfactory.

Candidates who received the standing "good" in religion, language, arithmetic, geography, history and natural history (or instead of the last three a foreign tongue) at the first examination or the final examination, and who, at the final examination, received the same mark in all subjects are legally qualified to teach in the lower classes of middle schools, and higher schools for girls.

TENTH CHAPTER.
NORMAL SCHOOLS FOR FEMALES.*

As is well known the number of male teachers in Prussia greatly exceeds that of the female. In 1886, 64,750 regular teachers were employed in the public elementary schools, and of the number only 6,848 were females. The ratio of female to male teachers varies greatly in different parts of the kingdom. In Protestant districts men are quite generally preferred even in the lowest primary grades. In ungraded schools the prejudice against female teachers is particularly strong both with Roman Catholics and Protestants.

There has been a great change in public opinion as regards female teachers within the past thirty years. In 1861, only 1,752 female teachers were employed in the public elementary, middle and high schools for girls. May 20, 1886, 6,848 were employed in the public elementary schools alone. These female teachers were very unequally distributed. Four thousand two hundred and thirty-three were Roman Catholics, 2 551 Protestants and sixty-four belonged to other religious denominations. In the province of Hohenzollern only four female elementary teachers were employed; in Posen only thirty-six, while in Rheinland there were 2,855 and in Westphalia 1,206. In 1890 in the Landkreis of Aix-la-Chapelle, where inhabitants are mostly Roman Catholics, 120 females and 162 males are employed in one school commissioner district.

Ample provisions are made for the training of male teachers. Almost all engaged in elementary schools are normal graduates. The women are not so fairly dealt with. There are about twelve State normal schools for males where one exists for females. In Prussia girls do not receive much encouragement, comparatively speaking, to go on beyond the elementary school course.

November 15, 1888, there were nine State normal schools for female elementary school teachers in Prussia, with an attendance of 586. Two hundred and ninety-eight were boarding students; 288 were day pupils. There were also three training schools for governesses, and a number of private institutions for the preparation of female teachers.

We glance briefly at one of each of these public institutions at Droyssig.

Both institutions are boarding schools, the tuition and living expenses at the former costing sixty dollars annually with extras amounting to between sixteen and eighteen dollars; at the latter ninety-three dollars annually with extras from eighteen to twenty-one dollars.

---
* The salaries paid female teachers in rural schools vary from $250 (1,000 marks) to $500 (2,000) marks with rent, fuel and, in most cases, a garden.

Candidates for admission to the normal school for female teachers must have the same qualifications, except in music, as those for admission to other normal schools. In addition they must have taken a course in industrial training for girls. A beginning is desired in French, singing and playing upon the piano.

Candidates for admission to the normal school for governesses must have had preparation equivalent to that given in a good high school for girls, including the course in industrial training.

Candidates for admission to both these institutions should not be under 17 nor exceed 24 years of age. Formalities for admission are very much the same as in the case of normal schools for male teachers.

The course in the normal school for female teachers embraces two years, the pupils being divided into two classes; the course in the normal school for governesses covers three years, the pupils being divided into three classes. The number of pupils in the former institution is fixed at forty, that in the latter at forty-two.

At the close of the courses examinations are held, the successful candidates of the former institution receiving a license to teach in an elementary school; those of the latter a license to teach in a private school as governess or in middle and higher schools for girls.

ELEVENTH CHAPTER.

EXAMINATION OF FEMALE TEACHERS.

Female teachers are not subjected to a second examination as male teachers are.* There are two kinds of examinations for female teachers: (1.) Those held upon graduation from the normal schools at Berlin, Münster, Paderborn, Posen, etc., or other institutions duly authorized. (2.) Those held twice a year in each province for candidates not trained in normal schools or other institutions authorized to hold examinations, *sub* 1.

Candidates must be at least 18 years of age.† They must be of good moral character and in good physical condition.

Application must be made not later than four weeks in advance, and candidate must state whether she applies for license for elementary or middle and higher schools, the two examinations being held together.

The following are to be submitted:

1. An autobiography upon title-page of which the full name of candidate, with place of birth, age, religion and place of residence, are stated.
2. Certificate of baptism (birth).
3. Certificate showing previous preparation and standing attained in examinations.
4. Certificate as to moral character.
5. Certificate as to physical condition.

---

* After an experience of five years in teaching, female teachers are admitted to the examinations for licenses to direct public and private schools for girls. "Fünfjährige Lehrthätigkeit berechtigt die Lehrerinnen zur Zulassung zu einer weiteren Prüfung, auf Grund deren sie die Befähigung zur selbständigen Leitung von öffentlichen und privaten Mädchenschulen erlangen." (Drs. Schneider and Petersilie.)

† As previously noted, male candidates must be at least two years older.

The examination is both theoretical (oral and written) and practical. The written examination consists of a theme in German, work in arithmetic and French; also, for license to teach in middle and higher schools for girls, English.

Applicants for licenses to teach in elementary schools are not forced to pass an examination in French.

The work is selected by the commissary of the provincial school consistory upon recommendation of the committee. In addition to the said commissary, the committee is composed of from three to five government officials, school directors or high school and normal school teachers, appointed by the government president of the province. The work selected should be comprehensive in character. In translating into or from a foreign tongue, the dictionary may be referred to.

The examination should be finished in one day. It should not last more than seven hours.

Before the beginning of the examination candidates must submit proofs of penmanship, using both Latin and German scripts, and a specimen of drawing.

The oral examination is held in the presence of the whole committee. It embraces methods and school management and all compulsory subjects taught in elementary or middle and higher schools for girls.

The practical test should be given, if possible, in a school of the same class as that for which applicant desires a license. At all events the subject must be one included in the course of study for such a school.

The subject for the practical test should be announced not later than twenty-four hours before the class exercises take place.

A written analysis of the work to be done in each class exercise must be submitted.

Candidates for licenses to teach in elementary schools must have the following qualifications:

1. In Religion (not given).
2. In Language. Familiarity with the method of teaching reading, and the principal points in method of teaching correct oral and written expression of thought; some knowledge of master-pieces in poetry and a closer acquaintance with the best literature for the young. Candidates must be able to state clearly, both orally and in writing, subject-matter connected with the elementary school *curriculum*.
3. Arithmetic.* Facility in the solution of problems in mental and written arithmetic; knowledge of common and decimal fractions and the different processes used in business transactions; computation of areas of surfaces and contents of solids; acquaintance with methods of teaching and ability to explain the same.
4. History. General knowledge of the principal facts and events in universal history, more particular knowledge of the same in German history, and a thorough and connected acquaintance with Prussian history.
5. Geography. In addition to particular knowledge of the Fatherland, general knowledge of the political geography of the globe and

---
* *Rechnen* includes both arithmetic and algebra. *Arithmetik* also, used in a general sense, includes algebra.

the principal points in physical and mathematical geography. The candidates must be acquainted with the use of atlases, globes, tellurians, etc.

6. Natural history. Knowledge of the important types and families in the three kingdoms, also cultivated and poisonous plants, especially those of the home. Clear insight into a botanical system, general knowledge of the other systems of classification, including the elements of geology. The candidates must be acquainted with the most useful objects in teaching natural history, such as charts, etc.

7. Physics and chemistry. A knowledge of the elements of these subjects gained through experimentation.

8. Pedagogics. Knowledge of the fundamental principles of education and instruction; acquaintance with the subject-matter of some of the principal works in pedagogics, and the lives of prominent educators of the last 300 years.

9. Vocal music. The singing readily and in good form of a school, religious and national song at sight, and knowledge of method of teaching singing.

10. Drawing, gymnastics and industrial training. An understanding of methods of teaching and objects used in teaching.

11. French (voluntary). Correct pronunciation, knowledge of the principal grammatical rules, ability to translate an easy selection from French into German, and *vice versa*.

Candidates for licenses to teach in middle and higher schools for girls (*Mädchenschulen*) must have the qualifications under 1, 3, 5, 6, 7, 8, 9, 10, and in addition:

1. Language (German). Ease and correctness in oral and written expression of thought; a knowledge of general national literature and literature for the young; comprehensive knowledge of the master works in poetry, acquaintance with the various forms of prose and poetry and usual meters; a thorough understanding of the method of teaching reading and the principal grammatical rules and methods of teaching general language work.

2. French and English. Correct pronunciation; knowledge of grammatical rules and their applications; ability to translate readily the authors read in the course of study for middle and higher schools for girls; general knowledge of the literature of the languages.

3. History. Knowledge of general history; more particular and connected knowledge of German, especially Prussian history.

A record of the standing of applicants in each subject is kept. Certificates are given in accordance with the general result. Applicants for elementary schools must attain at least the mark "sufficient" in religion, language and arithmetic; those for middle and higher schools, in addition, the same mark in French and English.

TWELFTH CHAPTER.
SPECIAL CERTIFICATES.

No person can teach in a Prussian public or private school, or in a family, without authorization from the government. In addition to the licenses for regular teachers, there are special certificates for particular lines of work. Such are given to teachers of drawing, male and female; teachers of gymnastics, male and female, teachers of music, male and female; female teachers of industrial training for girls; teachers in deaf and dumb asyla and institutions for the blind, etc.

With the exception of industrial training for girls, all subjects in elementary schools are very generally taught by the regular teachers. The other special teachers are those for drawing, music and gymnastics sometimes engaged in elementary schools in large cities.

Applicants for admission to the examination for these special certificates must either have passed the regular teachers' examination or prove, in addition to the technical knowledge required, that they possess the necessary general qualifications.

May 20, 1886, there were 34,270 teachers of manual training for girls engaged in Prussian elementary schools. Of this number, only 5,496 had passed the special examinations provided for such teachers; 26,091 of those who had not passed said examinations were employed in rural districts, and were, as a rule, the wives of the regular teachers. In 1886, the instruction given in this department cost $600,626. The average salaries paid were about eleven dollars annually in the country and forty-nine dollars and a half in the cities. As will be seen, teachers of manual training for girls have little opportunity of growing rich by their profession.

There are special technical schools and special courses in normal schools to prepare teachers for particular lines of work, such as drawing, music, manual training, gymnastics, etc. There are also special courses to prepare candidates for the examinations for teachers and directors in middle schools.

Special certificates in France are better arranged than in Prussia. The time has come in New York for special certificates for excellence in particular lines of work, such as penmanship, drawing and industrial training. Special teachers should not be required to pass the regular examinations for the higher grades. In addition to the technical knowledge, the general requirements for temporary licenses are sufficient, and special teachers who possess them should not be subjected to oft-repeated examinations.

THIRTEENTH CHAPTER.

SCHOOL COMMISSIONERS.

(KREISSCHULINSPEKTOREN.)

The following regulations for the Regierungsbezirk of Dusseldorf, concisely stated, will serve as a definition of the position and duties of *Kreisschulinspektoren* or school commissioners.*

School commissioners, in their respective districts, must watch over all educational institutions, both public and private, committed to their charge. They must see that all decrees be enforced, and that, both with teachers and pupils, patriotism and loyalty to the reigning

---

*In cities, the *Stadtschulinspection* performs the duties of the *Kreisschulinspektor*. According to decree of 1881, the reports of the *Stadtschulinspection* should be submitted to the *Kreisschulinspektor*. He forwards same to government. Decrees from government are forwarded through the *Kreisschulinspektor* as well.

family be aroused and developed. Over the school commissioner stands the government; upon an equality with him, the Landrath, and beneath him school boards, local school inspectors, directors and teachers.

RIGHTS OF THE SCHOOL COMMISSIONER.

1. To pass judgment upon proposed alterations in school-houses and new school buildings; to have a hearing in all disciplinary cases affecting the industry or character of his teachers.
2. In all business matters in his sphere of action, either through the Landrath or directly, to make proposals and offer explanations to the government.
3. In proper cases, to seek the assistance of the Landrath.
4. To require the assistance of local authorities in matters pertaining to his office.
5. To be present and preside at meetings of school boards.
6. In accordance with regulations, to grant his teachers fourteen days leave of absence.
7. To be present and preside at all public examinations of educational institutions in his charge.
8. To supervise all said institutions as directed hereafter.

DUTIES OF THE SCHOOL COMMISSIONER.

I. As Regards Alterations of Districts, Repairs and Play-grounds.

1. When the school commissioner learns the advisability of altering a school district or forming a new district or new classes, he must consult the local school inspector and board of education, and after thorough investigation, submit propositions to the Landrath.
2. To see that boards of education make necessary repairs and provide properly for the play-ground and gymnastic appliances. His directions must be carried out unless, upon appeal to the government, this is deemed inadvisable.

II. As Regards the Attendance of Pupils.

He must note carefully the attendance of pupils at every visit to each school under his jurisdiction. He must ascertain the reasons for irregular attendance. Whether this be through the direct fault of teacher in failing to punish the absentees, abuse of the power of granting excuses or other cause, he must seek to regulate the same, with the assistance of the Landrath.

III. As Regards The Visitation of Schools.

He must visit each class in every school under his jurisdiction at least once a year. He must examine each class to decide if same be doing the work required, reporting the result to the government.
Special attention should be paid to the following points:
1. Proper classification of graded and ungraded schools; due separation of the sexes in mixed schools.
2. Neatness, system and thoroughness in teachers' records.
3. Neatness of copy-books and other blank-books used for written work; proper oversight of teachers as regards the same.

4. Good arrangement of all written work; system and gradation in the same, preventing mechanical repetition.
5. The accomplishment of the work laid down for each class methodically and systematically.
6. The development of patriotism and loyalty to the government.
7. Proper discipline, neither too lax nor too severe.
8. The use of duly authorized text-books; to see that all children be supplied with the same.
9. To note that the necessary school furniture be on hand and that same be in good condition; that the school-room be clean, the windows whole and the walls properly painted or whitened.
10. To see if school-houses and out-buildings are in need of repairs; if the closets are well situated and kept clean; if play-ground answer all requirements and be provided with gymnastic appliances.
11. To note the behavior of the children outside the school premises.
12. To ascertain whether teacher be furnished with residence or pay rent for the same; whether teacher receive sufficient salary; the reputation of teacher in the district.
13. To ascertain whether the local school inspector fulfills his prescribed duties; his relations with teacher and reputation in the district; whether the school records kept by him are in order.
14. To ascertain if a school library be on hand and if same be furnished with good books; if not, to take steps toward providing for the same.
15. To ascertain if there be a *Fortbildungsschule*,* and if so, the attendance upon the same.

Information under 12 and 13 should be requested privately and only from reliable persons.

IV. AS REGARDS THE TEACHERS AND OTHERS UNDER HIS JURISDICTION.

The school commissioner should endeavor to secure the coöperation of his teachers and all school officers by justice and strict impartiality in all his dealings with them, and by a kind interest in their welfare. He should seek to carry out those measures his duties dictate, as regards teachers, local school inspectors and boards of education, rather by the exercise of persuasive reasoning than by the authority of his office. Recourse should be had to compulsion only when other means have failed and circumstances demand the recognition of his authority. He should sympathize with his teachers in all their joys and sorrows. He should ever be ready to give advice and help when called upon. His judgment of teachers should always be marked by strict impartiality. Finally, he should do his utmost to encourage the advancement of teachers in their chosen profession through conferences, reading circles and other institutions to perfect their knowledge and teaching capacity.

V. AS REGARDS VACANCIES, SUBSTITUTIONS AND HALF-DAY SCHOOLS.

When a school or class becomes vacant, it is the duty of the school commissioner to provide a substitute as soon as possible until the appointment of a new teacher. Should expenses arise in carrying out

* Schools for youthful workmen and apprentices.

this provision, the Landrath should be notified, that same be covered. In the case of a school with more than one department, when no substitute is at hand, it may be necessary to establish for a time, according to regulations, the *Halbtagsschule* (half-day school). If in the case of a school of one department no substitute is at hand, the school commissioner either provides himself as best he can for the emergency, or advises the government of the case at once.

VI. AS REGARDS THE WIDOWS OF TEACHERS.

The school commissioner must, so far as possible, and in accordance with decrees, look out for the families of deceased teachers.

VII. AS REGARDS PERIODICAL REPORTS.

The school commissioner must make, in the month of May each year, a full report to the government, through the Landrath, showing the condition of education in his district. In many parts of the kingdom other officers are appointed to perform the duties of school commissioners. There are special regulations for reports made by such officers.

VIII. AS REGARDS RECORDS.

The school commissioner must keep the following:
1. Copies of all general decrees relating to his work.
2. A register of acts relating to each school under his jurisdiction.
3. A journal of official correspondence received and answered, and all official documents.
4. A record of visitations, with remarks thereon. The forwarding of these records may be demanded by the government. In addition, each school commissioner must present annually a journal of his official travels, showing the number of nights he has been forced to sleep away from home, the number of days spent in traveling, the distance traveled, and whether by railway, steamship or public highway.

ANNUAL REPORT OF SCHOOL COMMISSIONERS.

These reports cover, 1, alterations in districts; 2, reports of local school inspectors; changes in local school inspectors; manner in which their duties are performed; 3, reports of school boards; care of schools under their jurisdiction.

Statistics required are as follows:
a. The number of schools, classes and pupils at the close of the year.
b. The classification of these schools.
c. The number of Protestant, Roman Catholic, simultaneous* and Jewish schools and classes.
d. The number of classes of boys, of girls and mixed classes, both generally and according to religious confession.
e. The number of *Halbtagsschulen* and *Halbtagsklassen*, that is, half-day schools and classes.

---
* Simultaneous schools are schools in which Roman Catholics and Protestants are educated together.

f. The number of Protestant, Roman Catholic and Jewish pupils, and the division of the same according to sex.
g. The number of classes and especially the divisions of the ungraded schools with eighty pupils, from eighty to 100, exceeding 100.
h. Increase or decrease in figures of previous year from *c* to *g.*
i. Number of schools or classes not in session.
j. Condition of school buildings, school furniture and teacher's utensils; improvements in the same.
k. Health conditions in the school, regulations affecting the same.
l. Changes in system, combinations of small schools, mixing or division of the sexes, etc.
m. The school districts, circumstances; needs of the same.

Statistics as to Teachers.

1. The number:
   a. Of Protestant, Roman Catholic and Jewish teachers in the public elementary schools in the district at the close of the year.
   b. Of the Protestant and Roman Catholic teachers in simultaneous schools.
   c. Of schools which became vacant during the year; for which teachers have been found; remaining vacant.
   d. Of old teachers who have received new positions, and of new teachers, with the religious faith of the same.
   e. Increase or decrease from previous year in number of Protestant, Roman Catholic and Jewish teachers.
2. The work of schools preparatory to the normal.

Attendance, Etc.

1. Conditions of attendance; obstacles in the way of regularity; reasons for unexcused absences; means to promote regularity.
2. Instruction given; conditions of the same; a general and particular report.
3. Interruptions through sickness of teachers or other cause.
4. School government and discipline, including religious exercises in schools and the attendance of pupils at church.
5. Patriotic and other school festivals; the part taken by the district upon such occasions.

Teachers.

1. Work in and out of school; number of cases teachers have been disciplined by the government; cases of discipline of pupils by teachers; the number of cases teachers have been dropped, stated separately with reference to decree concerning the same; testimony as to recent graduates of normal schools and other new teachers.
2. Principal and assistant teachers; their relations to each other; the mutual relations of assistant teachers.
3. Kind and number of teachers' conferences, work done by the same; libraries for teachers; condition and use of the same.
4. Extra work done by teachers; preparation of candidates for normal schools and other private teaching; work as organist or sexton, as conductor of vocal societies, treasurer of certain funds and agencies, occupation in arboriculture, culture of bees, etc.

5. Financial matters; salaries of teachers, benefits, endowments, widow and orphan pensions and insurance societies for teachers.

PRIVATE ELEMENTARY SCHOOLS.

1. Number of Protestant, Roman Catholic, simultaneous and Jewish schools and classes; also the systems as regards classification at close of year;
2. Number of pupils in attendance altogether and in accordance with religious faith;
3. Increase or decrease in one and two from previous year;
4. Courses of study and organization of these schools; conduct of teachers employed.

HIGH AND OTHER SCHOOLS NOT DIRECTLY UNDER THE GOVERNMENT.

1. Number of schools, classes and pupils at the close of the year as follows:
 a. The public and private schools;
 b. The Protestant, Roman Catholic, simultaneous and Jewish schools;
 c. Schools for boys, for girls, mixed schools;
 d. Number of pupils in the above according to religious faith and according to sex.
2. Organization: The number of boys' schools following the course of study of the Gymnasium, the Realschule and the middle school; the systems of classification of girls' and boys' schools; the teachers employed.
3. Changes in organization and new arrangements.
4. Boards of education and those paying for maintenance of the school; relations of the same to the school.
5. Attendance.
6. Instruction; conditions of the same; general and particular report; school books.
7. School government and discipline; devotional exercises in school; church attendance of pupils.
8. Patriotic and other school festivals; part taken in the same by the public.
9. Work of the teachers in and outside school; relations of teachers to other officials of the school; extra employment of teachers; conferences.
10. Condition of school buildings and teaching apparatus; increases and improvements in the same.
11. Financial conditions; teachers' salaries, benefits, endowments, stipends, etc.

If institutions have printed course of study a copy of the same must be forwarded with report.

12. Number of *Fortbildungsschulen** and *Kleinkinderschulen*† and number of pupils in attendance; increase or decrease from previous year; condition and work done by these institutions.

---
* *Fortbildungsschulen* are schools for young workmen and apprentices. These schools go on with elementary school work, taking up especially those lines which will be of practical use to pupils learning trades.
† *Kleinkinderschulen* are *Kindergärten* and other institutions for children under school age.

SUPERVISION OF SCHOOLS IN JANUARY, 1889.

The government districts (*Regierungsbezirke*) in Prussia are subdivided into school-circles (*Schulaufsichtskreise*). A government official is charged with the supervision of the common schools in these school-circles, either as his sole occupation or in connection with other duties. In the majority of cases, school-circles correspond with political-circles. Nevertheless, this is so arranged that Protestant and Roman Catholic schools have generally inspectors of their own religious faith. To insure this, school-circles are often formed according to dioceses.

The conditions of supervision in 1889 ("*Preussische Statistik 101*") are given in the following table:

SCHOOL-CIRCLES.

	As principal occupation of supervising officer.	As secondary occupation of supervising officer.	Together.
Number of school-circles	240	946	1,186
Number of school-districts	11,700	19,665	31,365
Number of schools	13,683	22,510	36,193
Number of classes	30,846	51,013	81,859
Number of public schools	13,052	21,429	34,481
Number of private schools	631	1,081	1,712
Number of Protestant schools	4,265	19,725	23,990
Number of Roman Catholic schools	8,731	1,368	10,099
Number of Jewish schools	148	203	351
Number of simultaneous schools	539	1,214	1,753
Number of Protestant teachers	8,401	42,186	50,587
Number of Roman Catholic teachers	18,280	4,392	22,672
Number of Jewish teachers	235	338	573
Total	26,916	46,916	73,832

The next census will be taken in November, 1890, but full statistics of the Prussian elementary schools will not be published in all probability before 1892. The last census dates from December 1, 1885. Full official statistics based upon this census were not published until 1889.

It is to be noted that in the matter of supervision, Prussia lacks uniformity. A large proportion of the school-circles come under the jurisdiction of government officials who are charged with other work in addition to that of supervising the schools.

School commissioners, having no other occupation, have been appointed in districts where two languages are spoken, in East and West Prussia, in Posen, Schleswig-Holstein, in the government districts of Aix-la-Chapelle and Oppeln, in school-circles where the matter could not be intrusted advantageously to other officials, and, in general, where the government felt anxious to raise the standard of primary education.

The government officials, charged with the supervision of the schools as a secondary occupation, are generally clergymen, in the country, and school-councilors or city school inspectors in the cities. This is the case in Königsberg, Danzig and Berlin (here eight city inspectors assist the school-councilors), in Breslau, Liegnitz, Erfurt (here the municipal government supervises the schools), in Altona, Kiel, Hanover, Cassel, Frankfurt am Main, Wiesbaden (here the city *Schuldeputation* supervises the schools), in Barmen, Crefeld, Düsseldorf, Elberfeld, Cologne, Duisburg (here there is a special *Stadtschulinspection*)

Occasionally school-circle supervision is intrusted to a director (*Rector*) as in Dortmund ; a normal school director as in Dillenburg ; a government school-councilor as in Trèves.

The school-circles (*Schulaufsichtskreise*) are again subdivided into school districts under the supervision of local school inspectors, generally the clergyman or mayor. Often, however, the local inspection is done directly by the school-circle supervising officers. In 1889, school commissioners (*Kreisschulinspektoren*) were charged also with this local inspection in the case of 7,084 schools.

Although all officials with duties similar to those of school commissioners (*Kreisschulinspektoren*) are highly educated and have passed through a long period of training for their work, yet the lack of uniformity in the appointment of school-circle supervising officers is a great disadvantage.

The annual outlay for government supervision is as follows :

Salaries of government councilors and helpers	$99,534 52
Salaries of school commissioners (*Kreisschulinspektoren*)	284,872 86
Salaries of other officers with duties similar to those of school commissioners	125,595 24
Appropriation to raise the standard of inspection in West Prussia, Posen and Silesia	47,619 04
	$557,621 66

School commissioners (*Kreisschulinspektoren*) receive at first $600 (2,400 marks) annually, with an allowance for rent and fuel, and $300 (1,200 marks) for traveling and other expenses. The salary of $600 increases gradually with the years of service.*

FOURTEENTH CHAPTER.
TEACHERS' CONFERENCES.

These may be classified as follows:
1. Those held once a month, excepting July, for all teachers of a city school (Berlin) under the direction of the principal. These are held outside of school hours.
2. Those held eight time a year, or, if possible, once a month, in conference districts embracing fifteen teachers. The meetings are

---
* The average salary of school commissioners is $886.97, with an allowance for rent and fuel, and $300 for traveling and other expenses.

presided over by the school commissioner. The conference lasts generally one day, sometimes half a day.

3. Those held once a year by normal school faculties with teachers in neighboring schools. The conference lasts one day (decree of September 20, 1880).

4. Those held at least once a year in each school commissioner district, under the direction of the school commissioner. Conference lasts also one day.

In all cases attendance is compulsory, and, in the last three, schools are closed to afford teachers the opportunity to attend. In the last two cases, allowances are made to cover traveling expenses, and special railway tickets are issued. A record of the attendance and work done is made in each instance, and the record is submitted to headquarters.

At these conferences, class exercises are held, methods of teaching are discussed, school organization, classification and discipline receive attention, the decrees of the ministry touching public education are announced and explained, and questions of general interest to educators are debated.

I attended several of these conferences, and was much impressed by the depth of thought in the papers read, the addresses and discussions. Vocal and instrumental music are prominent features at these meetings. Imagine an orchestra of twenty or more pieces, wholly composed of teachers, and able to play difficult classical music. I heard such orchestras several times.

The principal conferences generally conclude with a large dinner, which adds not a little to the prevalent feeling of good fellowship among the teachers. The funny man is always there. For many weeks he husbands his resources to make a hit upon this occasion. At one of the last conferences I attended, he produced what he called a "*Drehlied.*" This was a song composed by himself and printed within concentric circles. While the circles were large, the teachers did well, but as they grew smaller, the paper could not be turned fast enough, and all became very dizzy in attempting it.

FIFTEENTH CHAPTER.
SCHOOL DISCIPLINE AND MISCELLANEOUS REGULATIONS.

The teacher in Prussia has much more authority over his pupils than the teacher in New York. He exercises this authority both in and out of school, and it covers, also, children of other classes than his own in the same school, but not pupils of other schools.

Corporal punishment is allowed, but same must not be carried out to such an extent that the health of the pupil suffer in consequence. If the pupil be too severely dealt with, the teacher is disciplined by the *Provinzial-Schulcollegium*. Very severe cases subject teachers to fines of 300 thalers* or imprisonment for three years. If the injury be permanent, the teacher is imprisoned for five years in a penitentiary or for one year in a State prison. The former confinement brings

---
* A thaler is equal to 71.4 cents.

with it generally the loss of citizenship. Ordinary imprisonment does not necessarily involve these consequences. Imprisonment from two to ten years follows in cases where injuries were given intentionally.

If death result from injuries received, the person inflicting these injuries is imprisoned not less than three years in a house of correction (*Zuchthaus*) or three months in a State prison (*Gefängniss*). Circumstances under which the injury was given receive careful attention.

Fines, up to 2,000 thalers for the benefit of the person injured, may be inflicted.

An official, teacher or other employé of the government, who, in the exercise of his office, inflicts or permits the infliction of serious injuries, is imprisoned for not less than three months. If there are extenuating circumstances, the imprisonment may be shortened to one day or a fine of 300 thalers. If the injury be exceptionally severe, imprisonment for two years follows. Extenuating circumstances may limit this imprisonment to three months.

The following decrees regulate the infliction of corporal punishment by school teachers:

1. Corporal punishment should be resorted to only when other disciplinary means have failed, and then only in cases of obstinate persistence in lying, great stubbornness and disobedience, gross immorality and persistent lack of industry.

Teachers are not permitted to form the habit of resorting to corporal punishment daily and hourly. When possible, little children and girls of all ages should not be punished in this way.

2. In the case of little children less than 9 years of age, the teacher must use a light switch; in other cases, a pliant stick not thicker than the little finger may be employed.

3. Girls are to be hit upon the back alone, boys upon the back or the *Gesäss*. The force of blows must be moderated. In inflicting corporal punishment the clothing must not be removed.

4. The use of a thicker stick or rule, hitting with hand, fist or book in the face and head, hair-pulling, ear-twisting or that of other parts of the body, punching in the breast, back and head, or other like punishments, are forbidden.

5. Pupils are not to receive corporal punishment while at their desks, but in an open space of school room. It should be administered at the close of the recitation hour, never in the hour devoted to religious studies.

6. Switch and stick should be in teacher's closet during the hours for instruction, not directly at hand.

7. The grounds and extent of the punishment inflicted must be recorded in the teacher's register.

8. In cases requiring very severe measures, whether faults were committed on or off the school premises, the teacher should notify the local school inspector and inflict the punishment in his presence. In large schools such matters are brought before a conference of the teachers, and the punishment is inflicted in presence of the director (*Rector*).

9. When teacher has been too severe in inflicting corporal punishment, he is disciplined by the *Provinzial-Schulcollegium*. Serious cases

subject him to penalties fixed by the penal code. School inspectors must forward well grounded complaints, even though injuries inflicted be not serious, to the *Provincial-Schulcollegium*.

10. Teachers often found guilty of excess in inflicting corporal punishment, in addition to the other penalties, forfeit, for long or short periods, the authority to inflict corporal punishment

11. To lessen complaints brought against teachers, disciplinary measures should be often discussed, and all teachers, especially the younger, should study thoroughly the decrees relating thereto.

It is to be noted that no actions against teachers can be brought, either in civil or criminal courts, except in cases where a child has received some real bodily injury, wound or bruise. This is also the case when local school inspectors and school commissioners have inflicted corporal punishment.

A glance at the regulations for pupils in higher schools shows that they are closely watched at all times:

1. If the school director ascertains that pupils are living in a *pension* which he deems unsuitable, it is his duty to notify the parents or guardians of such pupils. If no attention be paid to this notification, the pupils are expelled.

2. Pupils from other districts can not select nor change their boarding-place without the authority of the school-director.

3. Pupils from other districts are under the special oversight of the *Ordinarius*.

4. Pupils who absent themselves from the city or village over night, even though they lose no study or instruction-hour, must have the permission of the *Ordinarius* or school-director. This applies to pupils from other districts not dwelling with parents.

5. Pupils must have permission of *Ordinarius* or school-director to attend theaters and balls. Pupils residing with their parents at home must procure the permission of parents to attend theaters, and can only attend public balls in the company of parents or guardians.

6. Pupils who give private lessons must procure the permission of *Ordinarius* or school-director.

No outsider is permitted to enter or disturb a public school under five thalers fine or imprisonment.

Teachers must be on hand fifteen minutes before school opens. Tardiness should be closely watched.

Children may not be kept at school so as to lose midday meal, nor should they be kept after school until dark.

Children are not permitted to give presents to teachers, nor are they allowed to take up collections.

Children under school age are not allowed to be present in the school-room during school sessions. The teacher is not permitted to wear slippers during school-hours.

The pupils are forbidden to frequent taverns, confectioneries, saloons. They are not allowed to attend dramatical, musical and acrobatic performances, except in the company of parents or guardians. They are encouraged to protect useful animals and government property, such as railways and telegraph lines. They are warned against the careless use of fire-arms.

Teachers should watch over the private reading of pupils. They should be protected from obscene literature.

Children of school age are not allowed to peddle; to sing or play upon any musical instrument in the street; to declaim in the street or take part in any dramatical performances. Those who take dancing lessons or set up ten-pins may not be kept out later than 10 o'clock in the evening. Proprietors of public places are forbidden to permit the frequentation of children of school age, and to give or sell to such children spirits or beer.

OBSERVATIONS.

Visitors to Prussian elementary schools will often notice slight transgressions of the disciplinary regulations, such as ear-pulling and the like (*vide sub* 4). Teachers thoroughly understand how far it is safe to go without danger of being reported to headquarters. The regulations give them a field which, according to our ideas, is, to say the least, broad enough.

Discipline is certainly far better, generally speaking, in German than in French schools. This may be attributed to the difference in the French and German characters. Many find an explanation in the abolition by law of corporal punishment in French schools.*

SIXTEENTH CHAPTER.
APPOINTMENT OF TEACHERS.

The following regulations concerning the appointment of teachers are taken from the decrees of the government at Düsseldorf:

The power of appointment to a newly created position or a vacancy is vested in the government. Boards of education recommend three candidates, and if one of the three be a suitable person for the place, he is appointed. No position may be filled without the decision of the government. This rule applies also to assistant teachers.

I. VACANCY OCCASIONED BY DEATH OF TEACHER.

1. The board of education (*Schulvorstand*) must give notice to the school commissioner (*Kreisschulinspektor* or *Stadtschulinspection*) with date of death and proposal for temporary substitution. The same notice must also be served on the *Landrath*, that proper provision may be made for teacher's family.

2. The school commissioner must report to the government without delay the fact of the vacancy, stating provisions made by him for temporary substitution. He must also inform the *Landrath* who the temporary substitute is and whether costs arise from substitution.

3. The *Landrath* should then endeavor, so far as same lie in his province, to regulate the payment of deceased teacher's salary to the family for the month of death, and a month of grace, where costs have arisen, or for the month of death and three months' grace where there are no costs.

II. VACANCIES ARISING FROM OTHER CAUSES.

4. Teachers are permitted to abandon positions only at the close of a term and after three months' notice. The shortening of the term of three months can take place only with consent of the school board,

---
* In France, Italy and Belgium, corporal punishment is forbidden by law. As Buisson said in 1875, the precision of the Prussian disciplinary regulations shocks us.

and through the school commissioner and *Landrath*, the government. This permission will not be granted unless provisions are made to carry on the school without interruption.

5. The notice is to be given in writing by teacher to school board; by school board to school commissioner and *Landrath* without delay. If change has not been directed by the government and therefore known, the school commissioner must notify the government directly. The *Landrath* proceeds at once to provide for the regulation of teachers' accounts, that if possible the same may be closed at his departure.

6. Teachers prepared in the state normal schools and under the jurisdiction of the government district of Düsseldorf are obliged to *remain in the same position to which the government has appointed them a period of three years.* Within this period they have no authority to give notice of change, unless directed by the government to do so.

III. THE FILLING OF VACANCIES THROUGH DULY AUTHORIZED TEACHERS.

7. So soon as a position becomes vacant through death or other cause, the school board (*Schulvorstand*) advertises the fact in, at least, the official paper. Three weeks thereafter the school board decides upon the three names to be presented to the government. Within three days the names of these three candidates with certificates and biographical sketches must be forwarded to the school commissioner. In exceptional cases, the government extends this period of three weeks.

The names of candidates must be given alphabetically, and opposite each name the statement whether candidate assumes a definite or provisory position.

In case less than three candidates apply, this fact is to be stated.

8. The school board may express a preference for some particular candidate, though this does not interfere in the least with the power of appointment vested in the government, and may not be considered.

9. The school board must forward propositions, names of candidates, certificates and biographical sketches to the government through the school commissioner and *Landrath* without delay. School commissioner and *Landrath* may express opinions as to propositions made. Care should be taken that all this matter reach the government within eight days from date notice was forwarded to school commissioner by the school board.

10. In case no candidates apply within the time stated, the school board notifies the government through the same officials, abandoning the right of proposing names or stating proposed steps in case time be extended.

11. School boards are obliged, under penalties, to transact this business within the time fixed. School commissioners must notify the *Landrath* of fruitless attempts to do so. If within six weeks from date of vacancy the government has received no proposals, the vacancy is filled by the government.

12. All proposals must be without conditions. It is not permitted school boards to engage for a certain definite time or provisionally. The nature of the engagement rests with the government.

It is to be noted that the provisional engagement of a teacher does not last longer than six years, according to law. Consequently a teacher once engaged definitely can not be reëngaged provisionally unless through fault he has lost the right to definite engagement or abandons himself this right in seeking a new position.

13. In appointing a teacher the government fixes definitely the time he is to take charge of his new position and enter upon his new duties. The date of entrance upon discharge of duties must be reported in each case by the board of education to the school commissioner, and by school commissioner, through the *Landrath*, to the government.

IV. THE FILLING OF VACANCIES TEMPORARILY THROUGH CANDIDATES.

14. It is contrary to law to fill vacancies by candidates who have not passed the teachers' examinations. Such may be employed temporarily, with permission of the government, when there are no duly authorized teachers at hand. In each case a biographical sketch with official certificates as to character and qualifications is to be submitted to the government through the school commissioner. These cases are exceptions and occur only when the efforts to secure duly authorized teachers have proved fruitless and the government has made no provision therefor.

15. The employment of these candidates is only authorized under the oversight and responsibility of a duly authorized teacher. It is regarded as an experiment and is always subject to annulment by the school commissioner without notice. Regular contracts can not be made with these candidates. They receive a written statement of their duties and salary from the school board, with the condition that they may be dismissed at any time by the school commissioner, but that they themselves must give at least six weeks' notice before abandoning their work.

16. Dismissal of such candidates rests with the school commissioner who is forced to report to the government in each case.

V. SUBSTITUTES DURING VACATIONS AND LEAVES OF ABSENCE.

17. This is regulated by the school commissioner and school board. Expenses arising therefrom are settled with the assistance of the *Landrath*.

Regulations for other government districts are substantially the same.

SEVENTEENTH CHAPTER.
LEAVES OF ABSENCE OF TEACHERS.

The following is a brief statement of the rule for the government district of Düsseldorf:

1. Schools may be closed or sessions shortened by teachers without the express permission of the proper authorities only in cases of sudden illness or other necessary cause, and then said authorities are to be notified at once.

2. Permission to close schools or shorten sessions should never be granted without good and sufficient reasons.

3. The *Lokalschulinspektor* (local school inspector) has authority to grant a leave of absence of from one to three days. When more than one day, the school commissioner must be notified.

4. The school commissioner (in cities the *Stadtschulinspection*) has authority to grant a leave of absence of from four to fourteen days. The local school inspector, except in most pressing cases, must request this permission in writing and await a written answer.

5. The government alone has power to grant a leave of absence exceeding fourteen days. Requests therefor must be submitted by the local school inspector through the school commissioner and *Landrath*, both of whom must give their opinion of the matter.

6. Requests for leaves of absence on account of sickness must be accompanied with statement of physician as to patient's condition.

If permission is requested to visit some *sanitarium* away from home, the official physician of the district must certify as to the necessity therefor.

7. Request must contain information touching provisions for subtitute during the leave of absence. Unless said provisions are satisfactory, the leave of absence will not be granted.

In most pressing cases, the local school inspector may arrange for substitute or for close of school during leave of absence.

8. Leaves of absence when school should be in session for the purpose of consulting members of the government upon various school matters should not be granted as a rule.

9. The leave of absence can not begin before the receipt of permission. At its close the teacher must report to the local school inspector. Said official is to notify the school commissioner in case the bounds of the leave of absence be overstepped. The school commissioner notifies the government through the *Landrath*.

10. Leaves of absence from the district during vacations require no notification, unless absence is to exceed three days, in which case teacher is to notify the local school inspector, giving particulars.

11. Fixed penalties regulate the transgression of these rules by teachers.

12. The government may grant leaves of absence up to six months in case of sickness. Districts must pay costs for substitution.

Regulations for other government districts do not differ essentially from those for that of Düsseldorf.

CONCLUSION.

The superiority of the Prussian system of elementary education, as compared with that of New York, may be summed up in one sentence. *Prussia sends all her children between fixed ages to school, and protects them while there from the imposition of bad work.* Frederick the Great aimed to accomplish this in 1763. From his day the system has been perfected gradually, and stands to-day without a rival.

Since 1871, France has followed in the footsteps of her rival, and the standard of work done in elementary schools has advanced with a rapidity which seems almost incredible.

In 1888, the cost of public education in Prussia, including the secondary, trade schools, technical schools and universities, was reckoned at $1.7717 *per capot* of total population. Allowances for rent and fuel slightly increased these figures. Army and navy schools were not included.

The cost of public education in New York in 1888 (census of 1880) was figured at three dollars and eight cents *per caput* of total population.

Every impartial person must admit that Prussia secures in good results the full value of the money expended, and that New York does not.

The methods in use in Prussia can not be adopted as a whole in New York. This is clear. Nevertheless, wise legislation would secure for us similar advantages, as the example of France, a sister republic, demonstrates.

Our model elementary schools would then become the rule, and not the exception, as at present.

NOTE TO PAGES 29 AND 30.

According to the decree of March 31, 1882, Prussian High Schools are divided as follows:—

1. *Gymnasialanstalten* — { *Gymnasien.*—Nine years' course.
   Progymnasien.—Seven years' course. }
2. *Reallehranstalten* — { With Latin { *Realgymnasien.*—Nine years' course.
   Realprogymnasien.—Seven yrs' course. }
   Without Latin { *Oberrealschulen.*—Nine years' course.
   Realschulen.—Seven years' course. } }
3. *Höhere Bürgerschulen*—Without Latin.—Six years' course.

Wiese's most valuable work "*Verordnungen und Gesetze für die höheren Schulen in Preussen*," published in two volumes at Berlin in 1886 by Wiegandt and Grieben describes these High Schools in full.

As stated on page 29, the principal divisions are *Gymnasien* and *Realgymnasien*.

Gymnasien: The latest official course of study, as given on page 29, shows the following changes:—

Religious Instruction,	19	instead of 20 hours weekly.
Language (German),	21	" 20 "
Latin,	77	" 86
Greek,	40	" 42
French,	21	" 17
History and Geography,	28	" 25
Mathematics,	34	" 32
Natural History,	10	8
Physics,	8	6
Penmanship.	4	6

Progymnasien: These are *Gymnasien* without *Prima*, or the last two years. The course is seven years. The advanced class fits for *Prima* in *Gymnasien*.

Realgymnasien: The latest official course of study, as given on page 30, shows the following changes:—

Religious Instruction,	19	instead of 20 hours weekly.
Language (German),	27	" 29
Latin,	54	" 41
Mathematics,	44	" 47
Natural History, Physics, Chemistry,	30	" 34
Penmanship,	4*	" 7
Drawing,	18	" 20

* According to Wiese this should be 4 instead of 5 as given on page 30.

Realprogymnasien: The relation between *Realgymnasien* and *Realprogymnasien* is the same as that between *Gymnasien* and *Progymnasien*.

Oberrealschulen: The following is the list of the subjects studied and the weekly division of time:—

	(1)	(2)	(3)	(4)	(5)	(6)	(7)	(8)	(9)
Religious Instruction,	3	2	2	2	2	2	2	2	2
German,	4	4	4	3	3	3	3	3	3
French,	8	8	8	6	6	5	5	5	5
English.	-	-	-	5	5	4	4	4	4
History and Geography,	3	3	4	4	4	3	3	3	3
Mathematics,	5	6	6	6	6	5	5	5	5
Natural History,	2	2	2	2	2	3	-	-	-
Physics,	-	-	-	-	-	4	4	3	3
Chemistry.	-	-	-	-	-	-	3	3	3
Penmanship,	2	2	2	-	-	-	-	-	-
Drawing,	2	2	2	2	2	3	3	4	4
	29	29	30	30	30	32	32	32	32

Instruction in singing and gymnastics corresponds with that given in *Gymnasien*.

Realschulen: The relation between these schools and *Oberrealschulen* corresponds generally with that between *Progymnasien* and *Gymnasien*.

Höhere Bürgerschulen:—The following is list of subjects studied and weekly division of time:—

	(1)	(2)	(3)	(4)	(5)	(6)
Religious Instruction,	3	2	2	2	2	2
German,	4	4	4	3	3	3
French,	8	8	8	6	5	5
English,	-	-	-	5	4	4
History and Geography,	3	3	4	4	4	4
Mathematics,	4	5	5	5	5	5
Natural History,	2	3	3	3	5	5
Penmanship,	3	3	2	-	-	-
Drawing,	2	2	2	2	2	2
	29	30	30	30	30	30

Instruction in singing and gymnastics corresponds with that given in *Gymnasien*.

Gymnasien proper fit for the universities; the other high schools, for professional technical schools, for a business life and for learning a trade.

INDEX

A.
	PAGES
Acknowledgments	1
Algebra	51, 58, 65
Alphabet method forbidden in teaching reading	16, 33, 40
Apparatus	18, 20, 32, 33, 39, 44, 45, 57
Arithmetic	17, 34, 41, 51, 58, 65
Area of window openings at least 1-5 of floor space	24
Average experience of elementary teachers	49
Average number of pupils falling to one teacher	27

B.
Blackboards	20, 26, 33, 39, 44

C.
Chemistry	51, 59, 66
Children under 12 forbidden to work in factories or mines	4
Children between 12 and 14 restricted to six hours a day	4
Children, number of school age in public and private schools	7
Children, total number of school age	7, 8
Children foreign, number attending public elementary schools	16
Compulsory education laws	2, 4, 7, 8, 81
Conferences of teachers	74, 75
Corporal punishment in Prussia	75-78
Corporal punishment forbidden in France, Italy and Belgium	78
Cost of public education in Prussia	12, 13, 81, 82
Cost of industrial training for girls in Prussian elementary schools	67
Courses of study	2, 8, 9, 31-49, 49-52, 55-60
Course of study for ungraded schools	8, 9, 32-37
Course of study for schools with two departments	38-43
Course of study in schools preparatory to the normal	50-52
Course of study in normal schools	55-60
Cubic feet of air, *minimum* of for each pupil	24
Cultivation of a taste for good reading	17, 33, 34, 40, 50, 58, 65
Cousin, report of	2, 3

D.
Deaf and dumb asyla	29, 31
Dialects	15
Disadvantage of unequal distribution of population in New York	27
Disciplinary regulations	75-78
Distance of pupils from their schools	27
Drawing	18, 19, 34, 41, 42, 51, 52, 59
Dullards, school for	2

E.
Elementary schools, maintenance of the State's first duty	2
Elementary schools must not be closed in time of war	2
Elementary schools, *minimum* of instruction in	2
Elementary school teachers and clergymen freed from payment of taxes	2
Elementary school teachers have 6 weeks' instead of 3 years' military service	2

PAGES
Elementary schools, eight alphabets are taught in.................................14
Examinations............................4, 5, 6, 8, 29, 49, 53-55, 60-63, 64-66, 67
Examination of females for licenses to direct public and private schools for girls.64

F.
Females may begin teaching at 18...64
Floor space, *minimum* of for each pupil......................................23, 24
Fortbildungsschulen..6, 72
French...52, 60, 61, 65, 66

G.
Geography...17, 34, 35, 42, 51, 55, 59, 65, 66
Geometry...34, 41, 51, 58, 59
German script..13-15, 32
German language used since April 1, 1889 in teaching all subjects except
  religion...15-16
German script a barrier between Germany and other civilized nations.........14
Gymnasien..6, 29, 49, 53

H.
Half-day schools...38, 48
High schools..6, 12, 29, 30, 49, 53
History...17, 35, 42, 51, 55, 58

I.
Industrial training for girls..................................18, 36, 43, 66, 67
Insane Asyla...2, 29, 30
Institutions for dullards...2
Institutions for the blind..2, 29, 30
Institutions for children under school age.................................27, 28
Institutions for children of school age......................................28-31
Interest of the general public in school work....................................20

K.
Krippen..27
Kinderbewahranstalten...27
Kleinkinderschulen..27, 72
Kindergarten..28, 72
Kindergärten are private institutions in Prussia.................................28

L.
Language used in teaching foreign children...................................15, 16
Language work.....................13, 17, 33, 34, 40, 41, 50, 51, 54, 58, 61, 62, 65
Latin..29, 30, 56, 60, 61
Laws to lighten the burdens of local taxation.................................11, 13
Leaves of absence of teachers..80, 81
Leaves of absence of 3 days or less granted by local school inspector..........80
Leaves of absence up to 14 days granted by school commissioner................81
Leaves of absence up to six months granted by government......................81
Libraries for teachers..20
Libraries in normal schools...57
Libraries in preparatory schools...50, 51

M.
Males may begin teaching at 20...60, 64
Male elementary teachers are normal school graduates........................52, 63
Mathematics...17, 34, 41, 51, 58, 65

PAGES
Middle schools..2, 5, 29, 30, 49, 53
Music..17, 18, 35, 36, 43, 52, 60

N.

Natural history..17, 34, 35, 42, 43, 51, 55, 59
New school buildings..26, 27
New York elementary school system, inferiorities of................2, 3, 4, 81, 82
Normal divisions of elementary schools..31, 49
Normal schools..2, 5, 52-60, 63, 64
Normal schools for females..63, 64
Number of boys in middle and high schools..30
Number of girls receiving a secondary education..30
Number of school age in public elementary schools..7
Number of school age in private schools, middle schools, &c..7
Number of cases of truancy..7
Number excused through lack of school accommodations..7, 8
Number excused for other causes..7, 8

O.

Orphan asyla..29, 30
Orthography now taught dates from the school year, 1880, '81..15
Overcrowded school-rooms..26, 27

P.

Patriotism..19, 35, 42, 67
Pedagogics..53, 57, 58, 66
Penmanship..14, 15, 33, 40, 51, 55, 59
Pensions of teachers..2, 11
Percentage of foreign children in Prussian elementary schools..15, 16
Percentage of male and female teachers..48, 63
Phonetic spelling..15
Physics..51, 59, 66
Physical training..18, 36, 43, 52, 59
Play-ground..23, 25
Practice schools..53, 55, 57
Preparatory schools..2, 5, 49-52
Promotions in graded schools..9
Prussian schools not to be confounded with other German schools..1
Prussian elementary schools are free..10, 11
Prussia is divided into 14 Provinces..1
Prussia has no code of public instruction..1
Prussian gradations of public instruction adapted to political divisions..1
Prussian elementary school system, superiorities of..2, 3, 81, 82
Prussian compulsory education laws..2, 4, 7, 8, 81
Preussische Statistik 101, the latest complete official statistics..7
Private schools..8, 29
Privies..25, 27
Progress made in French schools since 1871..81, 82
Pupils division of according to religion..22, 48
Pupils, division of according to language..15, 16
Pupils, division of according to sex..48
Pupils must learn to read and write the Roman script..13-15, 33, 41
Pupils have six months' practice upon entering school in reading and writing the German script..32

	PAGES
Pupils excused through lack of school accommodations	7, 8
Public instruction must be secured against all casualties	3

R.

Ratio of male to female teachers	48, 63
Realgymnasien	6, 29, 30, 49
References	1
Reformatories	4, 29, 30
Relative distribution of Prussian elementary public schools	48
Religion, division of children according to	22, 48
Regulations fixing limit of pupils in each class	26, 27, 31
Religious instruction	21, 22
Religious instruction is compulsory	21
Religious instruction is impartial	21
Religious instruction, summary of decrees relating to	21, 22
Results obtained in ungraded schools	9

S.

School age	4
School buildings	25, 26
School commissioners, qualifications of	3, 5, 6
School commissioners, regulations concerning	67-75
School commissioners, rights of	68
School commissioners, duties of	68-72
School commissioner's order alterations, and repairs	68
School commissioners visit the schools	68, 69
School commissioners regulate attendance	68
School commissioners provide substitutes	69
School commissioners make periodic reports	70
School commissioners keep certain records	70
School commissioners preside over conferences	74, 75
School commissioner districts vary in size	6
School commissioners, salary of	74
School desks	25, 26
School-house site	23
School libraries	69
School-rooms	23-27
School records	33, 39, 45
School supplies	10, 11, 20, 32, 33, 39, 44, 45
Schools, normal divisions of	31-48
Schools, relative distribution of	48, 49
Schools opened from 1886 to 1888	49
School terms and vacations	9
Schools with one department	31-37
Schools with 2 departments	38-43
Schools with 3 classes and 2 teachers	43-45
Schools with 3 classes and 3 teachers	45
Schools with 4 departments	45, 46
Schools with 5 departments	46
Schools with 6 departments	47, 48
Schools, half-day (*Halbtagsschulen*)	38, 48
Scope of report	1, 2
Security of teacher in his position	2

	PAGES
Simultaneous schools	70
Special certificates	66, 67
State aid	12, 13
State supervision of private schools	3, 8
Supervising officers	6, 73, 74
Supervision of schools in January, 1889	73, 74

T.

Teachers, appointment of	78–80
Teachers' authority	75, 78
Teachers, leaves of absence of	80, 81
Teachers, power to appoint vested in government	78
Teachers' libraries	20
Teachers, qualifications of	5, 6
Teachers' wages	11, 12, 49, 53, 63, 67
Teaching a profession	3, 11
Text-books	19, 20, 33, 39, 45
Time pupils may work outside of school hours	32
Time-tables for ungraded schools	37
Township system	10, 27
Trade schools	12
Truancy, cases reported	7, 8

U.

Universities	6, 12

V.

Vacancies occasioned by death of teacher	78
Vacancies arising from other causes	78, 79
Vacancies filled by duly authorized teachers	79, 80
Vacancies filled temporarily through candidates	80
Vacations	9, 10, 57
Ventilation	24, 25, 26, 27

W.

Warteschulen	28
Windows	24

www.ingramcontent.com/pod-product-compliance
Lightning Source LLC
Chambersburg PA
CBHW032240080426
42735CB00008B/933